Tale of a multifaceted life
Volume 2
by Enice Toussaint

Éditions Nouveau Siècle

Éditions Nouveau Siècle

The "Nouveau Siècle (ÉNS)" editing house proposes heartfelt and personal works where freedom of expression comes first. In this day and age, despite all the conflicts, we are experiencing a world that is more unified. This is in large part due to telecommunications and a borderless global economy. This new form of reality facilitates exchanges between cultures and the conceptualization of a human identity finally in harmony with itself.

It is within such a vision of peace that this editing house intends to promote its activities: Publishing personal words, born of individual experience, wanting to testify to a world in transformation. To charge ahead into this new century, we must go forth without fear of change, of difference, of being yourself, of your thoughts and the thoughts of others. With such a philosophy, truewords, even the simplest ones, can help to nurture renewal within our world.

"Nouveau Siècle's" Mission Statement: To share thoughts and preserve memories...

Tales of a multifaced life written by Enice Toussaint.

It is the second Volume of four Volumes published by ENS Publishing

Éditions Nouveau Siècle.

For information, contact Natatsha Casimir

Visit our website: www.enspublishing.com

Email: ediontionsens@gmail.com

Project manager:

Natatsha Casimir

Book cover's conception:

Natatsha, Elle-Camay C. Reason and Max Casimir

Computer graphics of cover page: Elle-Camay C. Reason

Photography, Makeup: Natatsha Casimir

Conception of Internet site: Elle-Camay C. Reason

ISBN: 978-1-80623-714-2 -Print

ISBN: 978-1-80623-713-5 -ebook

Handing in – 2er trimester 2025

Bibliothèque Nationale du Québec

National Library of Canada -ebook

In memory of my mother.

For my children, Natatsha and Max,who helped me realize this writing project.

To my grandchildren, whom I adore.

May they cherish the memory of each life

and thus learn perseverance.

Your life can be filled with joys and satisfactions. We cannot allow obstacles to destroy well-being and happiness. We are defeated only if we accept defeat.

Martin Gray

The Book of Life

Table of Contents

Preface

In a simple, ordinary, and clear style, the Author presents their biography for the reader's attention. It is a captivating account based on real facts and events, presented in chronological order.

The description of the places is vivid, inviting the reader to take walks and engage in daydreaming. The characters are presented with human faces, highlighting both their qualities and their flaws, from which often emerge inexplicable practices and gestures.

Through their own life, the author describes the twists and turns of a woman in a relationship, more specifically the situation of a majority of voiceless women of all nationalities. It is a warning to this fundamentally sexist society, whose manipulations are barely perceptible.

This book opens a vast field of research and reflection for feminists and activists of women's liberation and empowerment.

D.M

Prologue

My Departure for New York

I am at Riverside Park in Manhattan. In front of me, across the river, is the city of New Jersey in the state of the same name. A boat full of tourists just passed by. I take a moment to enjoy the beauty of the landscape before I begin writing.

For a year now, I've been planning to continue my book: *A Woman Among Many Others*. I had intended to choose an inspiring place to do so. I was contemplating a trip to New York, and my daughter approved of the idea.

In reality, I was indecisive. I was also considering two other options: a trip to Haiti or a stay at a retirement home near Montreal. Ultimately, I chose the Manhattan district in New York City, the city of my dreams.

The departure had been delayed because I had other obligations in Montreal. My daughter's two children, Mikael and Sophia, were on vacation, as well as my little nephew, Steeve, who had come from Haiti for a two-month stay in Quebec. His mother had been the victim of a senseless crime in Haiti on December 31, 2003. In the family, it was mostly me who could free myself from my commitments. I had to change my plans to be there for the children. But I did not regret it. I enjoyed their company a great deal; it was, in fact, one of my most beautiful summers. I will cherish the memory for a long time.

At the end of the holidays, my daughter Natasha and I decided that it was time for me to leave for New York. Each week, I kept postponing my departure date. I felt very vulnerable and sad. I kept thinking, "Will I have the courage to leave everyone I love and go so far to write?" I remember how, when I wrote my first book, *A Woman Among Many Others*, I was full of enthusiasm and energy. I didn't shy away from any obstacles.

I did not reveal my anxieties to Natasha; I didn't want to worry her. I prayed to God, asking Him for the will, the audacity, and the inspiration. I prayed for three days; I even went to Notre Dame-du-Cap to meditate. I felt at peace and more determined. Two days later, I told my daughter that I would be ready to leave in two weeks.

I called my nephew Marco, who lives in New York (Manhattan), to let him know I would be arriving soon. I had already asked him, as well as his sister Valène, if they could host me for two months. Valène is rarely home; she works in New Jersey and comes home once a month.

The decision to write this book in Manhattan was, of course, because I love this neighborhood, but also because, since the events of September 11, 2001, every time I return there, I notice that a new miracle has occurred in the city of New York. It has become warmer; the people are more welcoming, taking the time to get to know their neighbors. A human side has taken root. I wanted everyone who doesn't know New York to come to appreciate it as much as I do. Because it is a magical city.

My Arrival in New York — September 24, 2004

My First Day in New York

With two suitcases and two small bags, I left Montreal on Thursday, September 24, at 11:45 PM, arriving at Port Authority in Manhattan the next morning, Friday, at 7:30 AM. My nephew Marco, who was supposed to greet me, wasn't there. However, his delay was very brief. After greeting each other, we took the Subway (the metro). The 42nd Street station was packed, and we had to walk a long way to get to the next one. Fortunately, a good Samaritan helped us.

Marco is my brother Alain's son. A very handsome young man, he is 35 years old. At the age of 15, he had to have one of his feet amputated. Stoically accepting his illness, he was the one who comforted his family from his hospital bed. He managed to finish his college studies and earned a degree as a social worker. He is currently working in his field. With his parents having returned to Haiti, he shares an apartment with his sister Valène. He is an extremely warm-hearted person.

Description of the Apartment and Neighborhood

The apartment is on the third floor of a building located on 104th Street, at the corner of Broadway, on the West Side.

It’s a large, very clean 4½ consisting of a spacious combined living room and dining area, a small kitchen, and two large bedrooms. Marco set me up in his sister Valène's room, which faces Broadway Street. From the room, I could see both streets, with passersby, especially on Broadway Street, though it was very quiet at night. Riverside Park is behind his place. What I particularly admire about this large Broadway Street is the presence of many fruit and flower shops, which add a unique charm to the area.

In the middle of the street, there’s a large flower bed that separates the two lanes; benches have been placed at both ends where people can sit and relax while enjoying a coffee. The neighborhood has everything: good restaurants, bars, churches. I was surprised by the number of churches in Manhattan; I will have plenty of options when the time comes to attend a mass.

After touring the apartment, I had a brief conversation with my nephew, then took a shower. Since I wasn’t hungry, I didn’t eat. I asked Marco what our plans were for the day, after which he left, probably to give me a little time to rest.

Since I hadn’t slept during the trip, I went to bed. I slept for at least two hours. When I woke up, I dressed and had a light snack. Upon Marco’s return, we went out. He planned to give me a small tour of the neighborhood. He accompanied me to St. Michael’s Church on Amsterdam Street, at the corner of 101st Street, but it was closed. We headed toward the one located at the corner of Amsterdam and 96th Street; it was open. We went in, and I said a prayer. On our way back, Marco pointed out the library located at 100th Street, at the corner of Amsterdam. I had a small craving, so I bought some plums, which I ate while walking around. I offered some to my nephew, but he didn't want any.

On the way back, we did some grocery shopping. Once back at the apartment, I felt too tired to prepare dinner. I gave Marco some money to buy prepared meals. Around 7 PM, I called my daughter and my sister to give them an update on my arrival. Marco came back with Chinese food, which we ate with pleasure.

My Second Day in New York — Saturday, September 25, 2004

Searching for the Best Places to Write

Marco and I left at 11:30 AM to return to the library on 100th Street; I planned to apply for a library card. They granted me one without any difficulty.

Description of the New York Public Library, located on 100th Street in Manhattan

It is an old, two-story library; the first floor is for adults, and the upper floor is for children. There is a small section dedicated to books in French. The librarians are very friendly. While observing the place carefully, I noticed a very quiet corner reserved for people who want to work in peace.

My Visit Continues

After leaving the library, we went to St. John's Cathedral, located at the corner of Columbus and 112th Street. It is a very beautiful and large historic church. Among other things, one can admire a monument made from debris of the two World Trade Center buildings from 9/11, in memory of the people and firefighters who died in the tragedy.

We then went to Columbia University. I was impressed by the grandeur and beauty of the university. I visited its library, and afterward, we retraced our steps to head to Riverside Park. Marco showed me the easiest route, which I would be able to remember more easily. We walked along Riverside Drive until 104th Street and then to Riverside Park. This, I thought, is exactly where I will come to write when the weather is nice. We continued our walk in the park for a few minutes, then we headed home. It was 4:30 PM. My day had been exhausting but productive.

I rested for a bit, then started preparing my writing plan. Around 6 PM, I prepared a light meal. After dinner, I called my sister and my children in Montreal to update them. Then, with my nephew, I watched a movie in the living room. I went to bed at 11 PM.

My Third Day of Exploration

Sunday, September 26, 2004

Having had difficulty sleeping, I woke up early. I walked to St. Michael's Church for the 11 AM mass. The mass is celebrated in the same way as in Catholic churches;

however, the Eucharistic part is placed at the very end. I found the hymns performed by the choir to be very harmonious and melodic. I was able to gather spiritually, which gave me a sweet satisfaction.

On my return from mass around 1 PM, I had lunch. Feeling tired, I rested for a bit. My niece Valène arrived at 4 PM; we were happy to see each other again. I complimented her on her weight loss. She returned the compliment, adding, "I think you've tanned like I did." I replied, "During the summer, you have to get some color; it's good for your skin." Since it was her birthday, I gave her yellow flowers that I had bought after leaving the church. Marco and I presented her with a greeting card. She seemed very pleased. We felt like having some wine. She sent her brother to buy some, but he didn't find any— the wine shops were all closed. Around 3:30 PM, we decided to have dinner outside and went to a Spanish-Chinese restaurant on Broadway.

Since it was Sunday, the restaurant was packed. We ordered our dishes. I personally chose fried plantains with shrimp and a salad. Valène had pork chops with a baked banana and salad, while Marco opted for beef stew. We also ordered a pitcher of sangria. The meal was very delicious and well-prepared. We were satisfied with the service. After finishing our meal, we took a walk down Broadway. After walking 16 blocks, we reached 90th Street, at the corner of Amsterdam, where there was a prayer gathering led by Father Darbouse for the Haitians affected by the Gonaïves disaster in Haiti.

We didn't stay until the end. On the way back, we walked down the large Amsterdam Avenue toward the apartment, window-shopping as we went.

When we arrived at the apartment, I went into my room. I thought, "I came here for a purpose, to write." I then sat at the desk, reviewed the plan for the book, my work schedule, and timetable. Feeling a bit nervous and anxious, I went to bed. I told myself, "Tomorrow, Monday, September 27, I will launch my action plan." I then prayed to God to give me the will and inspiration. My sleep was very restless.

By presenting this introduction to this book, I wanted to show the conditions in which I wrote the second volume, *"Tales of a Multifaceted Life"*. Starting tomorrow, I will directly address the second phase of my life, beginning in January 1975, when Jacques came to pick me up from the caregiver, Mrs. Delisle, in Sainte-Thérèse-de-Blainville, a village north of Montreal.

I will describe the powerful moments, both happy and sad, that remained unknown to those around me. This new testimony will be extremely important for my family. I have lived such a different life experience from my children! I expect these revelations to bring moments of joy and suffering, but I must share them. The night before I start my writing project, I slept very poorly: my sleep was filled with terrifying nightmares.

Upon waking, I still felt anxious and indecisive. I kept questioning the validity and timing of my project. Why all of this? Well, I must go for it! I need energy. I know I'm the only one who can provide it! I started praying. I asked God to send me an angel to inspire me with the strength, will, and inner peace I need.

I then closed my eyes to meditate. After asking myself many unanswered questions, I opened my eyes and saw the photos of my grandchildren on the desk. I stared at them for a long time. I felt like the children were speaking to me as I focused on those photos. I thought about them and their future.

Suddenly, an idea came to me. I thought, "Why not write my book as a long letter to my grandchildren in the form of a diary?" This way, I could converse with them, and through this letter, seek to instill the joy of life in them. They will accompany me through the great adventures of my past.

With this thought, I felt better, ready to begin my great dramatic and mystical journey with my grandchildren. I took my bag and went out of the building. Once outside, I took a long breath as I made my way to Riverside Park.

Tuesday, September 28, 2004

Chapter 1

January 1975

Back from Mrs. Bélisle's House, the Caregiver, after My Release

After having breakfast with Mrs. Bélisle and my children, I called Jacques to have him pick me up. "Where are you?" he asked. "I couldn't find you anywhere since yesterday!" I replied that I needed to be alone and, above all, I needed a mother at that moment. He simply responded, "Alright, I'll come get you."

When he arrived, I said goodbye to my children and Mrs. Bélisle, thanking her for everything she had done for me. Lost in my thoughts, I didn't speak much with Jacques during the ride. He took me to my sister's place and left immediately afterward to go to work. I felt happy to be at the end of this ordeal.

At My Sister Irène's House

I went to my sister's house, where I found her a little worried. "Maybe she feels too much pity for me," I thought. This assumption was based on her sharing some strange conversations she had had with Jacques. I thought it would pass, but I didn't know that during my stay at Mrs. Bélisle's, Tony had told her a completely made-up story about Jacques.

Apparently, Tony told my sister that Jacques claimed that, if he wanted to, he could also have sex with her and many other things! I don't know if Jacques had really made such claims because at that time, I didn't know him very well. Today, even though I'm not inclined to believe it, a slight doubt still lingers in my mind!

Tony didn't say anything negative about me because he knew that my sister had a deep affection for me. He was trying to win her favor. In any case, she would never betray me, so I advised her to ignore Tony's words and asked her to let me make my own choices. She didn't approve, but she complied with my wishes.

It was a Monday. I worked at night, so I had the entire day to sort out my thoughts.

The apartment wasn't very large: a kitchen, dining room, a bathroom, and a bedroom that was turned into a living room during the day. We made do. Since our brother Robert lived with Irène, we had very little space. However, the apartment was very clean.

Robert rarely spoke to me; however, he and my sister listened in on my phone conversations: they didn't like it when I shared my personal problems with friends. At the time, I found them quite suspicious, but I understood a few years later that they only wanted to protect me.

Around 10 PM, I went to my job, which was taking care of the sick at the Sisters of the Holy Name of Jesus and Mary House on Mont-Royal Avenue in Outremont. At the end of my shift, the director, Sister Monica, informed me that I would be working during the day starting the following Monday. I was very happy about that and thanked God.

Since my sister Irène and my brother Robert had always lived together, my arrival disrupted their routine a bit: I was encroaching on their space. Despite their affection for me, we didn't share the same lifestyle. They were quieter, more reserved; they didn't speak too loudly or make noise, while I am very open and expressive. I love to talk, discuss, explore all aspects of a subject, and live freely without too many complications. My way of living must have bothered them quite a bit.

However, Irène spoiled me a lot. Sometimes, to encourage me, she would pick me up in the morning after my shift when she had a day off. After having breakfast together, we would go to church. Everything went pretty well, but a certain discomfort remained because Jacques would often call or come pick me up to take me to a restaurant or somewhere else.

Many of my friends called me, came to visit, or invited me to the restaurant to discuss my problems, like Yvi's father and many others. Some had eventually taken Tony's side and no longer spoke to me, while others concluded that I had not made the right choice. I never showed those who ignored me that their attitude affected me: I didn't feel the need to.

I kept in touch with my lawyer. So, one day, when Tony called me, I told him, "If you have something to say, tell my lawyer." He didn't take it very well.

Meanwhile, the atmosphere at my sister's house gradually changed. Since I was now working during the day, I was able to rest better and felt less nervous. It was better for me because I wasn't getting enough sleep. As for the children, it was becoming clear that they were much better off at Mrs. Delisle's.

One morning, I had a very heated argument with my sister and brother. I was very angry. I slammed the door and left like a madwoman, not knowing where I was going. I cried bitterly.

I felt torn between Jacques, who wanted me to move in with him, and my sister, who tried to dissuade me, wanting to protect me. And I hadn't made a clear evaluation of the situation at that time. I acted like an adolescent who decides her own path. Now, I understand her. However, back then, I chose the solution of running away.

At My Cousin Gisèle's

I called Jacques to inform him that I would no longer be staying at my sister's, that I was at a restaurant, and that I would like him to come pick me up. Twenty minutes later, he was already there. His car was a red Volkswagen hatchback. He likes to drive very fast. With all these events, I felt as if I were in a cloud, like a spectator of what was happening to me. While waiting at the restaurant, I couldn't stop crying; it was stronger than me.

As soon as he arrived, Jacques asked me what had happened. I answered, "I left slamming the door. I don't know... that's all. Don't ask me for more." He didn't insist. He thought I looked very shaken. I told him I would ask my cousin Gisèle if it was possible for her to host me for a short stay.

He thought it was a good idea. I then revealed that Gisèle's apartment was small and that two of her friends were already living with her. "It won't be for long," he replied, "just until we find our own apartment."

I contacted my cousin, and she agreed to host me, offering me the sofa in the living room, if that didn't bother me. "That's fine for now," I said, "thank you. I'll come right away since this will solve my problem."

My cousin Gisèle is a very simple person. She is the daughter of my aunt Paulette, one of my father's sisters. She was the one who used to call me "Têt sèk" (short hair) when I was a child. When she arrived from Haiti, she stayed for a while at my sister's house on Saint-Denis Street (as I mentioned in my first book).

My cousin lived in a basement apartment with an open floor plan: bedroom, kitchen, and living room were all one space. I quickly realized that it wasn't the ideal living situation. The sofa wasn't comfortable. On the second night, Jacques also wanted to sleep on the sofa, but it gave way under our weight.

I talked about my situation with a person I had only recently met. She had started working at the same place as me and was named Anièce. She was a tall woman with remarkable qualities, including being spiritual and very meticulous.

The first time I saw her, she had simply greeted me. The next day, we got to know each other better. She was the mother of a little boy, and a few years later, she also had a daughter named Nadine, whom I saw being born. We became very good friends.

I told her that I urgently needed to find an apartment. She responded, "I have a friend who is leaving her apartment in two days. I'll call her tonight and give you news." I thanked her, telling her I was counting on her. I also informed Jacques. And I prayed to God to get that apartment.

In the meantime, I called my sister to apologize. I explained that I was staying at Gisèle's until I found a place. My sister responded coldly, but I understood. I told her that I would come pick up my things as soon as I had my apartment. I would call her every day to check on her, as keeping the family connection was important to me.

As for Jacques, he had to sleep at a friend's place since he had left Tony's. And I could never go live with him at his friend's house—never in my life! Jacques had to take responsibility, meaning he needed to rent an apartment, which he did.

Anièce eventually let me know that her friend would let me take over her apartment. It was located in Saint-Léonard, in a basement on Couture Street; it was a furnished 3½ apartment. I met the owner, who rented it to me without making me sign a lease. I called Tony to let him know I would be coming to pick up the rest of my things that same evening, just one more day! He couldn't refuse.

When I lived in Anjou with Tony, I had made friends nearby: Nélia and her husband Simon. Since I didn't want to go to Tony's alone or send Jacques there, I asked Simon to accompany me to get what belonged to me, and he agreed. I wanted to avoid any confrontation with Tony. I had left everything behind: furniture, TV, household appliances. Among the children's furniture was a bookshelf my brother had given me, and I was determined to get it back.

Jacques, who had arrived a few minutes earlier, was waiting outside. Upon entering the apartment, I met Tony's sister, Édith, his daughter Clarice, and Tony. I greeted them and took what I needed, then left. The whole thing lasted only thirty minutes. I thanked my friends for taking the risk of helping me. It's a moment of my life I will never forget. Tony was obviously very surprised to see me. He didn't say a word, and neither did I; I made sure not to provoke him.

Thus, my liberation from Tony was accomplished. There remained the procedures for the custody of the children and the divorce.

Through all this suffering, there is one thing I have never regretted: having had my son Max with Tony, because he is an adorable son.

Chapter 2

My First Apartment in My Life with Jacques

February 1975

Part One

That same evening, February 15, I took possession of the apartment, accompanied by Jacques. As soon as we entered, Jacques wanted to make love right away. "Now, it's done," he whispered to me, "I have you all to myself. I can make love to you whenever I want." I retorted that we both had to be consenting. He insisted. Since there was already a bed in the apartment, we eventually made love. He then fell asleep, and I stayed awake, reflecting on all of it. Then I thought to myself, "My son needs to come live with us here." After that, I started putting things in order. A little later, I took a shower and got ready for bed, but I had noted earlier that I would call Mrs. Bélisle to let her know I would come to pick up Max over the weekend.

My decision surprised Jacques. I made it clear that I was very serious. He then agreed that Max could come live with us. I then went to my sister's house to retrieve what I had left there. Despite everything, I still felt sad and fragile, not knowing why. As for Jacques, he was overjoyed!

He accompanied me to my sister's. She was in a bad mood; she didn't say anything, but I could sense her anxiety. Perhaps she was worried about me. We still had a sewing machine to retrieve. Jacques went up to the apartment to get it on his own. This time, my sister didn't let him in: she put him out. It was over. Looking back, she was right to act that way, after everything he had said about her.

They stayed at odds. On my side, I remained in contact with my sister, even though our relationship wasn't the warmest. I wanted to maintain my bond with her because I loved her very much.

We continued and finished setting up the apartment. Jacques worked from 7 PM to midnight, and I worked during the day, from 7 AM to 3 PM, which suited us well. In the mornings, he would take me to work, and he would pick me up at 3 PM.

He worked in a foundry in Saint-Léonard. The commute took 10 minutes. Jacques was full of energy. He always wanted to make love. He didn't need any foreplay to feel ready. He was like a machine. He would wake me up in the morning before going to work, and in the afternoon, he would want me again. I didn't understand what was happening. I was always exhausted, and I had no time for myself. At first, it was okay, but after a while, you start to ask yourself a lot of questions...

I couldn't wait to pick up my son. Max's arrival had been delayed by a week because of my work.

Second Part

My Place of Work

Life goes on. I call my sister every evening to check on her and my brother. For now, I avoid going to her house: I'm waiting for a noticeable improvement in our relationship.

My life is turning into a vicious circle: it's divided between my work, meal preparation, apartment maintenance, and sexual relations. It's excessively exhausting. At work, everything is going well. I take care of four patients. The patients like me. Sister Margherita and Sister Agate, who are my favorites, especially appreciate me. I became their ray of sunshine as soon as I entered their rooms. I love going to work; it's my time of rest and relief!

Sister Margherita was very plump. She had difficulty walking and had to use a "walker." She was ambulatory and had been a teacher before becoming a nun. She told me about her life, and I told her about mine. On my days off, she became sad; she would sulk at my replacement and make her work difficult.

When I entered her room, she would take my hand and kiss it. I was both tender and strict with my patients. By doing so, I managed to get even the most difficult ones to cooperate.

Sister Agate's younger sister, on the other hand, was delicate and very beautiful: she looked like an angel. She couldn't walk anymore and stayed in bed. Every afternoon, we had to lift her and sit her up for at least an hour.

When I entered her room in the morning, she expressed her joy with her eyes and hands. Her eyes sparkled like the blue sky, while her hands tried to say something that didn't come out of her mouth because she was voiceless. It was wonderful to see her. I would run my hand through her white hair like snow to give her some affection.

Another sister was a former school principal. She was very strict. She kept telling me over and over that she wasn't like the others, as she had once been a principal. I wasn't supposed to treat her like the others.

Sister Tessier was slim, haughty, and snobbish. She could move around, but still needed help. When I was on duty, she didn't want anything to do with the other staff. She would grumble, "I don't want anything from you all; I'm waiting for Miss Toussaint to return." Yet, she was a good person. I never had any issues with her. I knew how to approach her.

I always made a point of carefully avoiding bringing my personal problems to work. I knew that these patients needed tenderness and attention. Even if I felt sadness, as soon as I entered their rooms, I conveyed joy. It was necessary because they needed it.

I had every other weekend off. During one of those weekends, on a Sunday, we went to pick up Max. He and his little sister Natasha were very happy to see me. But Mrs. Bélisle was very sad because Max was going to leave her. However, the fragile health condition of Mrs. Delisle made this decision necessary. Despite her physical condition, she felt guilty for not being able to keep him. I reassured her by explaining that having Max with me would help me feel less lonely when Jacques went to work. Max, on the other hand, wasn't happy to return home. He would miss his little sister and Mrs. Bélisle as well. He still obeyed without complaining too much. After having dinner at Mrs. Bélisle's, we went back to Montreal.

We decided to set up Max's little bed in our room, which seemed very cramped to him. Melancholic, Max didn't speak much. I understood his sadness. I reassured him by saying not to worry, emphasizing that these arrangements were temporary, just until we found another apartment. He murmured, "Yes," with deep sorrow. Being separated from his little sister and confined to a small apartment! His situation caused me intense sadness.

One day, when I was off, I went to enroll him in the local school in Saint-Léonard for kindergarten. From then on, everything went smoothly: in the morning, Jacques would take him to school, and at noon, he would pick him up. On my side, I could enjoy some sexual relief: fewer intimate moments in bed at any time. Life followed its calm and peaceful course. My lawyer started legal proceedings for child custody and alimony. I was waiting for him to tell me the date of the hearing. On Mother's Day, after returning from work, I found a card from Tony in my mailbox. He hadn't made such gestures when we were living together. I didn't call him to thank him.

Every other weekend, we would visit Natasha in Sainte-Thérèse. She and Max were always happy to see each other on these occasions. He looked forward to that day.

We were looking for a bigger apartment. We found one in Anjou on Ronsard Street between Neuville and Chambeau, a large 3½ apartment, but unfurnished. So, we had to buy furniture on credit. And we had to enroll Max in a school in our new neighborhood.

Choosing furniture wasn't easy: every time I picked out a living room set, it was never the right one; Jacques always found a reason to reject my choice. If I picked a white or beige leather sofa, he preferred wine red. In the end, he convinced me that it was the best choice. For the bedroom and dining room, the same routine: his choice always prevailed, and I watched him do it without saying anything. For me, it was fine, that's all.

Part Three

At Court for Child Custody and Alimony

The court appointment was set for May 1975. Since I was living with Jacques, my lawyer warned me that I would need to present convincing arguments to obtain custody of the children. I had to demonstrate that Tony would not be a good father. He had asked for custody of the little girl, of whom he was the legal but not biological father, and he knew very well that he wasn't. He did this solely to hurt me. He had not requested custody of his own son.

I reassured the lawyer, telling him not to worry. I would have evidence. I prayed to God, asking for His help. I called my sister to warn her of the news. She was outraged, knowing that Tony was not a good father. She promised to be on my side. My cousin Vivianne said, "If you need witnesses, I'll be there." My adoptive mother, Sister Berthe, was also shocked. She assured me that I could count on her prayers and those of her companions.

And dear Mrs. Bélisle, when I told her the news, said, "Don't worry, I took care of those two children; I know who truly loved them and cared about them." She added, "Madame Enice, be at peace. I can give my name for the testimony in court." Usually, this woman is very gentle, but that time, I could hear the anger in her voice. It was as if her own children had been attacked. We were ready to launch the offensive, with the full support of God and the Virgin Mary.

Tony had hurt two mothers instead of one. I knew the battle would be tough, and I was extremely stressed. I no longer had any desire to make love. I pushed Jacques away; sometimes he would surprise me, and I would let him, but despite myself. The only thing that mattered to me was the fate of my children.

Finally, the big day arrived. I had taken time off work. Vivianne and Mrs. Bélisle accompanied me to court.

The hearing took place at the Montreal Courthouse on Notre-Dame Street. Upon arrival, I saw him with his lawyer. I didn't greet him. I hadn't seen him since our separation. He seemed surprised to see Mrs. Bélisle and Vivianne. The lawyers withdrew to discuss. I stayed with my friends. I was both very nervous and confident.

My lawyer, a tall Québécoise named Thérèse, was a very respectful person, but also self-assured. I felt safe having her as my lawyer.

The hearing was scheduled for 11 AM. The witnesses stayed outside the courtroom. Tony had no witnesses. When the judge entered, everyone stood up. A few minutes later, I was called to the stand. I felt strong; I looked Tony in the eyes while speaking to the judge, explaining how Tony had treated us when he lived with us: the mental cruelty he subjected me to, his indifference toward the children and me, despite everything I did for him. I spoke without giving his lawyer time to question me. This surprised everyone, including the judge. When I finished, his lawyer dropped his case: "I have no questions," and the judge adjourned the hearing until 1 PM.

I was exhausted but satisfied. My lawyer congratulated me on my performance and said luck was on our side. We went to the courthouse cafeteria for lunch. I took the opportunity to discuss my testimony again. I emphasized that we needed to stay firm because the battle wasn't over! Lunch was very pleasant.

At 1 PM, I returned to the courtroom. It was Tony's turn to testify. His lawyer asked him a question. He insisted on the fact that I was living with another man and that he wanted custody of his daughter. He almost repeated the same arguments I had just presented to the judge.

When my lawyer asked him to describe what kind of mother I was, he couldn't answer. He couldn't give a precise response. Then it was the witnesses' turn. Mrs. Bélisle was called to the stand. My lawyer asked her a question. With her usual gentleness, she described how I lived with the children and emphasized all the affection I gave them. But she also pointed out that Tony was always eager to return home when he came to see them. He showed them no attachment, no affection...

When Tony's lawyer tried to embarrass her with a tricky question, she responded: "These children are happy with me and with their mother." A man who abandons his work to avoid paying child support doesn't deserve to have custody of his children. After Mrs. Bélisle's testimony, the judge announced, "I don't need any more witnesses. I have everything I need. I'll take a 10-minute break."

For me, it was a win. I cried, and so did Mrs. Bélisle. My lawyer was pleased. Ten minutes passed. The bell rang to announce the return of the judge. My heart was pounding as the judge made his decision: "The petitioner will have custody of her two children, Max and Natasha. The little girl will be cared for by Mrs. Bélisle, and the father will have no right to visit her. As for Max, he will stay with his mother. The father will have no visitation rights. However, he will be allowed to pick him up every other weekend. Since Mr. [Tony] claimed that he doesn't work, the child support is set at twenty-five dollars per week. The petitioner has refused alimony for herself."

Chapter 3

July 1975 — Life in Anjou on Ronsard Street

Part One

Our new apartment on Couture Street (Saint-Léonard) wasn't very large, but it was quite comfortable. It was located on the ground floor of a building. We accessed it through a door at the back of the building, but we could also enter through the main entrance of the building. The children could play safely in the backyard. My friend Aniѐce came to help me settle in. We managed to do everything in one day. As usual, Jacques and I immediately made love in our new apartment. I had three days off for the move. On the third day, I rested.

Jacques was still working at the Galvan Métal foundry in Saint-Léonard. Since this job involved serious risks, Jacques was looking to change professions. Since my friend Dona worked at Canadian Steel Foundry on Notre-Dame Street, I asked her to make inquiries for Jacques. She suggested that he go there and fill out a job application form, mentioning his name as a reference.

And life went on. Max came back to live with us. We took turns taking care of him. Everything was going well in that regard. During his vacation, Max was happy to be alone with me. He could play in the yard. One evening when Jacques was away, the phone rang; while I went to answer it in the bedroom, I heard Max yelling, "Mammy, mammy, the pan is on fire!" I rushed out of the bedroom and to my great surprise, I saw flames shooting from the stove. Fortunately, I was able to quickly put out the fire with soda.

I was scared! The building's alarm went off, and the firefighters arrived. They broke open the kitchen cabinets to check if the fire had spread. Before leaving, they scolded me, saying, "Madam, you did a good job, but next time, call us!" The next day, the landlord had the broken cabinets repaired. When the fire started, my son looked at me with eyes full of fear. It was that look that triggered the appropriate reflex in me to put out the fire. Since that day, Max is afraid of fire. As for me, I learned my lesson: I never leave the fire on when I answer the phone.

Part Two

Our First Summer Vacation in 1975 with the Children

Vacation time had arrived. I chose the end of July for mine. We went to pick up Natasha from Mrs. Bélisle for these 15 days off. The children were happy. Natasha was two years old, tall for her age. She loved playing outside with her brother under my supervision. We had picnics at Cap-de-la-Madeleine, Côte-Sainte-Catherine, etc. We took them to La Ronde. They had a great time. The children were my priority. Jacques and I made love less often during that time, which suited me perfectly.

When the vacation ended, we took Natasha back to the caregiver, Mrs. Bélisle. She was thrilled to return to Mrs. Bélisle's because the house was bigger and she slept alone in her crib. Mrs. Bélisle surrounded her with affection. She didn't work; there was less tension in her home. It's not that I didn't show affection to my daughter, quite the contrary.

But since I worked a lot, I always felt tired. Working, making love almost all the time, taking care of the house and a man, it was really too much! It was better that my daughter live with this lady who loved her a lot.

It was August, a week after the construction holidays, and Canadian Steel had still not called Jacques to offer him a job.

Without his knowledge, I decided to call the company myself to get an update. I managed to speak to the HR manager, and I informed him that my husband had applied for a job a month ago but had received no response. After making me wait for two minutes on the phone, he told me that my husband could start working the next day at 2:30 PM. I thanked him and wished him a good day.

When Jacques returned, I shared the good news with him. He was overjoyed, but I don't remember him thanking me.

Third Part

Visitation Rights, Max at School

The judge had granted Tony the right to pick up Max every other weekend. He was supposed to call me to let me know the time and day he would come. One Thursday evening, he called to announce that he would pick up Max on Saturday morning at 10 AM and return him on Sunday. I reminded him that he had to bring him back by 6 PM. I also gave him instructions such that he would not be allowed to enter my house.

On Saturday morning, he did show up. Everything went well, but when Max returned from his father's, he was sad. I wanted to know the reason for his sadness. He replied, "He left me with people I didn't know." I reassured him by explaining that it was normal and that he wasn't supposed to get used to those people. The next weekend, when he returned, he confided, "He promised me toys. He didn't give me anything. I don't want to go back to his place." I told him that next time, he would at least get a toy. The third weekend, he came back crying again, saying, "I don't want to go anymore," he moaned. I replied, "It's the law, you have to go when he comes to pick you up." I don't know if God listened to his little prayer as a child or his suffering. The fourth weekend, he didn't come. And he never came back to pick up Max. He never called to ask about him, and he never paid child support. Max didn't understand why his father didn't come anymore, but he was happy not to have to go with him. He never inquired about Tony. That's how the child custody situation ended. But the divorce process was still pending.

Max at School

I had enrolled Max in a school near our home. Because of the distance from Jacques' workplace, he could no longer pick me up from work in the afternoon. I had to take the bus. In the mornings, Max would leave for school with the other children; in the afternoon, when he returned, he was looked after by a Quebec woman who lived in the same building, waiting for me to return. When I came home from work, I would pick him up, prepare dinner, help him with his homework, give him a bath, and put him to bed. He was 6 years old and in first grade.

Fourth Part

The Fire

It was May 1976. One day, Jacques called me at work to ask me to come home earlier because Max's caregiver was absent; he was going to leave Max alone for half an hour until I arrived. He told Max not to go outside and not to open the door for anyone. It was the beginning of spring, it had started snowing again, and it was cold. I returned as quickly as I could. Upon arrival, I saw that the building across from ours was on fire. I was terrified! They wouldn't let me enter the affected street. I shouted to the firefighters, "I live here!" I begged them, but without revealing that my six-year-old son was alone in the apartment. Eventually, they let me pass.

When I entered the apartment, I saw Max watching the fire from the window. I put his coat on, grabbed the papers I thought were important, and went outside to join the other tenants. While we were outside, my son looked at me with eyes like fireballs and said, "Mommy, did you see the fire? It's bigger than ours. I was scared." Taking a deep breath, he added, "You know, mommy, someone knocked on the door several times, but I didn't open it. I did the right thing, didn't I, mommy? You'll tell dad I listened to you." I kissed him and complimented him, "You did well, you're a brave little boy, I'm proud of you." He was very excited.

This fire incident deeply affected Max. Now that he's married and has children, he sometimes prepares dinner himself. He never leaves the fire on under a pot unattended. I am also aware that if my son had opened the door, and the firefighters had realized he was alone in the apartment, we would have had serious problems.

Since that incident, I never left Max alone again. If, one day, I couldn't find a caregiver, I stayed home. When I saw the building on fire, my heart nearly stopped because I thought the fire was at my building. I understood that God was teaching me to be cautious in life.

Fifth Part

Jacques' Sister's Arrival from Haiti — Her Stay with Us

For a year, Jacques had applied for residency for his sister Claudette, who lived in Haiti. Her request had been granted. A few months later, Claudette arrived in Montreal and came to live with us.

Claudette had no work experience except for sewing. But since she didn't know how to operate an industrial sewing machine, Jacques rented one so that I could teach his sister how to use it. Claudette wasn't progressing with her learning, so I decided to find her a "general job." I checked the classifieds. A candy store on Iberville Street was hiring, so I suggested this to Claudette. "Let's go apply for a job at this candy store. I'll present myself with your card. I'll submit the application for you, pretending to be you. If they hire me, you'll go work in my place."

And that's what I did. After the interview, the manager invited me to come work the next morning. I thanked her. The next day, Jacques' sister showed up in my place, following our plan. I did this, of course, to help her. Otherwise, she wouldn't have been able to work. I don't regret doing this for her.

Sixth Part

My Illness — My Hospitalization at Santa Caprini

One night, I woke up with intense pain in my stomach. I was having great difficulty breathing. I asked Jacques to take me to the emergency room. Seeing me in so much pain, he quickly did so.

Since my sister-in-law was still at the house, we left Max with her. Upon arrival at the emergency room, I was seen by a doctor without delay. He asked the nurse to give me a sedative, then added, "Prepare her for surgery; in my opinion, she has gallstones." Since they hadn't given me any x-rays, he couldn't actually know if his diagnosis was accurate.

I asked Jacques to verify things. I didn't want to undergo surgery without having tests first. The nurse gave me an injection. I asked her opinion about the doctor's decision, and she responded, "I'm not the doctor."

After the injection, I felt less pain. A few minutes later, the nurse handed me a basin. I passed a liquid stool mixed with small seeds that looked like stones. I had even excreted a few of them.

The doctor decided to keep me in the hospital. I then asked Jacques to go back home to check on things, call my employer to inform him of the situation, and take Max to school.

When Jacques returned to the hospital, I saw him enter with a hat on his head and a worried expression. He went to see the doctor and told him he didn't want his wife to undergo surgery without tests; otherwise, he would move her to another hospital. The doctor replied, "OK, sir, I will have her undergo x-rays; after the results, we'll see what we can do." Jacques then gave me a report on his conversation with the doctor.

A few minutes later, they indeed took me for tests, which revealed that my body had almost no stones left. I had eliminated a few in the stool, but as a precaution, the doctor decided to keep me in the hospital for further, more thorough tests to determine if surgery would be necessary. I was relieved that Jacques stepped in just in time.

I stayed five days in the hospital. A medication injection helped eliminate the remaining stones. Jacques came to see me regularly. But he complained that his sister wasn't helping him at home and that he had to do everything himself: the cleaning, the cooking, the laundry, taking care of Max, in addition to his job. He seemed discouraged.

Thus, my stay in the hospital would open his eyes to the extent of my daily tasks; at least, that's what I hoped. I also took advantage of my hospitalization to rest because I really needed it.

Seventh Part

The Incident One Evening

I remember an unfortunate event, one summer weekend, in our apartment on Ronsard Street in Anjou. One of my cousins, who lived in the United States, came to stay with us for two days. The apartment wasn't very big. We only had one bedroom. Max's bed was in the living room. That night, we offered our bed to the guest and we slept on the floor in the bedroom on an inflatable mattress, placed in front of the bed.

During the night, I felt a hand on one of my breasts. At first, I thought it was Jacques' hand. But I quickly realized he was sound asleep. And I immediately understood that it was my cousin who was touching me. I then jumped up and went to the bathroom to calm myself. His gesture had both surprised and shocked me. When I returned to the room, I switched places with Jacques.

The next day, our visitor could no longer look me in the eyes. Without Jacques knowing, I asked him the reason for his action. He gave me this explanation: "Enice, you know, ever since I was little, I loved you silently, without telling anyone." And he added, "I remember when I was young, I came to spend the summer holidays at my aunt's (your mother's) house; she was still alive, and you were young; I tried to tell you and show you my love for you. I realized that you didn't understand me. I didn't insist. Years passed, I could never tell you, and then I never saw you again, until today."

I replied, "You know, before doing something like that, you should have talked to me." He objected, "I was afraid of your response." I then shouted, "You want to know my response? I don't want to see you again! What you did last night was disgusting." Since that painful incident, I never saw my cousin again. I never told anyone about it, because the act was particularly shameful and vile. It made me realize that I should trust people less.

Conclusion of Chapter 3

I had great difficulty writing this chapter of my autobiography. The subject was complex! When I was planning the book, I hadn't included it because I had completely forgotten about it.

I had even forgotten the name of the street I lived on, and it took me nearly two days to remember it. I had tried to erase the event, but in vain! The characters followed me. I was forced to stop completely and restart everything a day later. It felt like I was climbing a steep hill. Finally, I made it through, and I'm relieved. I can now continue.

The incident coincided with the beginning of my life with Jacques. I found everything complicated and exhausting. His sister's arrival and my illness, all of it didn't help matters. We had to face too many trials at once.

Chapter 4

Plan to Find Another Apartment

Part One

My son needed his own room. I discussed it with Jacques, and he agreed that we should rent a new apartment. My friend Nélia had moved to Pointe-aux-Trembles on Baillargé Street. She gave me the contact details of the landlord. I called him to check and see if he had an apartment available for the first of July. He confirmed that, indeed, I could rent a 4 ½ for the proposed date.

Jacques and I went to visit the apartment on a day when I was off. It was perfect for us. It was located on the ground floor, with parking in the back for tenants. The emergency exit door and the balcony faced the parking lot. In addition to the main entrance door of the building, there was also a back door. The stove and refrigerator were not included.

We were very satisfied, especially since my friend Nélia lived in a 5 ½ on the second floor with her husband Simon and their children. We quickly signed the lease.

Over time, my sister and I became very close, and I often visited her with my son. Jacques didn't come with us; they were on bad terms. I understood. My sister didn't come to my house either. My brother Robert visited me occasionally. My sister didn't call me to avoid talking to Jacques in case he answered.

I had informed my sister that the apartment didn't have a stove or refrigerator. She told me that her friend Dédé wanted to sell his large two-door refrigerator at a very reasonable price. She then talked about our situation to Dédé. He sold us his refrigerator and lent us a stove until we could buy our own.

The landlord told us the apartment would be available from June 15. We planned to move on June 24. For such a move, we needed help. I asked my brother Robert, my friend Aniège, and Nélia's two boys if they would help us. They all agreed. Jacques had reserved a trailer for the move. We were ready for the move.

Part Two

Moving to Pointe-aux-Trembles, Baillargé Street. July 1976

On the morning of the move, my brother came to join us with his car, an AMC Hornet. With it, he could help Jacques transport the heavy furniture. I went to pick up my friend Aniège, who had promised to help. Since the cleanliness of the new apartment left much to be desired, we got to work as soon as I returned. Nélia's sons also came to help us. We had to hurry because Jacques and Robert would be arriving with their first load any minute. When they arrived with the furniture, at least the essentials were done. They were able to place them. We worked all day. By the early evening, the apartment was ready. Only a few details were left. I had prepared a nice dinner, which the whole team enjoyed. My brother then went back home, while Jacques took my friend home. Left alone at the house, I thought about my son. I thought, "Finally, Max has his own room, until his sister comes during my vacation or time off."

Our new neighborhood was very quiet. The only downside was the oil refineries nearby, on Notre-Dame East Street. The school was two minutes away from the house. Max was not in any danger, especially since my friend Nélia lived one floor up. Her children were older than Max. They could watch over him in our absence, which was convenient for us. The apartment, a 4 ½ with two bedrooms, was very spacious: we had a large living room, a kitchen, a dining room, and a large hallway. In the basement, there was a laundry room.

At the time of the move, the school year had ended. I took Max to spend a few days with his sister at Mrs. Bélisle's. Her absence would give us enough time to repaint and put the apartment in order. In the evening, we sat in the kitchen to have tea and plan for the painting, arranging the furniture, etc.

A little later, he whispered to me, "Now, it's time to go to sleep because we have a lot of work tomorrow. Don't forget that we need to baptize the room! Hmm! It's been so long since I've had you all to myself." After going to the bathroom, he got into bed while whispering, "Hurry up, I'm already ready." I decided to take a shower. I took my time. I was exhausted. Growing impatient, he yelled, "Even if I'm tired, I'm always ready. Don't forget that no one is going to come to your rescue." I replied, "Enjoy it; in a few days, Max will be back." He responded, "He has his own room now." After making love, he immediately fell asleep, but as usual, I couldn't fall asleep right away. I said my prayer, then went to watch TV in the living room to relax a bit. Eventually, I got into bed.

The next day was the painting day. Jacques and I did the work with the help of Nélia's children. In the evening, we arranged the furniture, put up blinds, and hung curtains. On Sunday, we went to pick up Max from Mrs. Bélisle's.

He was happy to see that he had his own room. I had put all his toys in there. He was overjoyed, especially when we took him to Nélia's. When he saw Nélia's children, he was amazed despite their age difference. He exclaimed, "Finally! I have friends, I can play." It was vacation time, so it was wonderful. The following Monday, I went back to work. Life continued.

I had requested to take my vacation starting July 15. So, I worked only two weeks. Life was calm. But in terms of our sex life, it became more intense than before.

I had already informed Mrs. Bélisle that I would come to pick up Natatsha during my vacation, before her birthday. We did just that. She cried when leaving Mrs. Bélisle's. But when she arrived at our house, she comforted herself by seeing her brother, with whom she would share the same room, and noticing the spacious apartment. On Natatsha's birthday, July 5, I organized a small party for her with Nélia's children and their friends. They were older. She turned three that day, and she was quite big for her age. For the occasion, I had prepared a pink and white cake, small snacks, pies I had made myself, juice, and milk. She always carried her rag doll under her arm and her favorite blanket. For the day, she wore a little yellow embroidered dress, white socks, and black shoes. She always wore orthopedic shoes or boots due to a birth defect in her left foot.

The little party went well, the children had a lot of fun. Natatsha was very happy with her gifts, my brother Robert had come to bring hers and those from my sister Irène. She was joyful with all the people she barely knew.

When she was with us, it meant more work for me, but everything was fine. Jacques worked a lot, and I did too. During our vacation, we had fun as a family. I had experienced some hair loss, so I had cut my hair very short (boyish). At the same time, we also cut my daughter's hair, because Mrs. Bélisle had trouble styling it.

The vacation over, we took Natasha back to her caretaker's in Sainte-Thérèse-de-Blainville. She seemed thrilled to see Mrs. Bélisle again. When it was time to leave, Max seemed sad to leave his sister. I understood him. This woman loved them a lot, and they loved her too. She had cared for Max since he was two years old, and Natatsha since she was two months old. She was the one who gave my daughter first aid and also the one who taught my son assurance, love, and tenderness. This woman had a warm personality. When I visited her, I felt good and at peace. She took great care of my children and gave them all the love they needed.

I loved them very much, too. But with the life I was leading, I couldn't give them, at their young age, the human warmth needed for their development.

I remember when Natatsha was one year old, she swallowed one of her small earrings. Mrs. Bélisle called me at work to inform me. She was worried about the child, and so was I. "I'm taking her to the hospital," she told me, "don't worry about coming, if there's something worse, you'll come, don't worry."

At the hospital, after the X-ray, the doctor saw the earring in my daughter's intestines. He asked Mrs. Bélisle what the child had eaten since the incident. She replied, "I gave her cereal in a bottle." He advised her to feed her solid food, like mashed potatoes. Which she did. During all the waiting, the little one didn't cry, while we were extremely anxious. She spent the night without going to the bathroom. The next morning, she was able to pass the earring. Mrs. Bélisle called us right away to share the good news. We were relieved. Since that day, Natatsha no longer wears earrings. I don't think I could have found a better person than her. That's why every day I have a special thought for this woman.

Part Three

Return to Work

At work, I was appreciated by the other employees and the patients on the floor where I worked. I formed a very strong friendship with a colleague named Edith; she was much older than me, and we got along very well. We took coffee breaks together. During breaks, she smoked (cigarettes), and most of the other girls also smoked. She insisted that I smoke as well. She would say, "Come on, try one, you'll see, it's really good, it'll make you feel better." I would always reply, "No." One day, she said, "Come on, try it!" I agreed. I smoked one or two cigarettes each day at work to keep her company. I didn't buy cigarettes because I didn't smoke at home. However, when Jacques smoked one, I would take a puff, no more. I remember one day, during the lunch break, she offered me a cigarette, and I refused. She insisted. I then revealed that I had stomach pain when I smoked. It was the truth. I was asthmatic. Every time I smoked, I had difficulty breathing. I never smoked again after that. The experiment lasted for three months. That was enough.

The Budget

At home, everything was going well. Jacques was very present. Sexually, he seemed very satisfied. He was always in a good mood. He also took care of the budget. I would simply sign my check and hand it over to him. He would accompany me to the grocery store and give me five dollars a week as pocket money. We had a joint account, but I could not make withdrawals without his permission. I accepted this arrangement as long as everything ran smoothly at home.

My main tasks consisted of taking care of him, having sex whenever he desired, taking care of my son, looking after the house, and going to work. I didn't think about myself first; I prioritized my marital duties, even if I didn't feel like it. I just did my best to satisfy him, nothing more.

I had started occasionally making cakes and pastries for friends, just to do them a favor. The word spread quietly, and gradually, I built a clientele. I made cakes for all kinds of occasions, and I also did hair and makeup for people on their wedding days. I worked a lot (I kept my job at the hospital). I was always tired, and Jacques, on the other hand, always wanted more bedroom sessions. For me, life continued as normal. I never revealed anything to anyone, and I never complained about the situation to Jacques.

Max's Birthday, November 1976

And Events at the Baillargé House

It was November 6, Max's seventh birthday. For the occasion, I planned a long weekend. We went to pick up little Natatsha.

I prepared a small party for Max. In addition to the cake and other treats, I had made little meat-filled puff pastries. The same friends attended the party. At seven years old, Max was still very mischievous. When we were in the car, despite my repeated warnings, he would unbuckle his seatbelt and his sister's. Jacques would then react by braking the car suddenly, deliberately. I remember once Max nearly hit the windshield. I yelled at Jacques, "Hey! If you keep driving this fast, we're going to have an accident!" He replied, "That will teach him to listen when he's spoken to."

Jacques' attitude baffled me: when something displeased him, he reacted aggressively. For example, one afternoon, he came to pick me up from work. I had delayed my departure by two minutes because the nurses' reports took longer than usual. I greeted him as I got into the car, but he didn't say a word. He started driving at full speed, and when I advised him to slow down to avoid an accident, he snapped, "I have the right to act as I please." And he accelerated even faster, like a madman. He was driving recklessly. I then told Max, sitting in the back seat, to "buckle up." But Max, being a child, found the situation amusing. I felt helpless, and my heart was pounding. Jacques didn't stop the car until we arrived home. I was terrified! I thought I was going to die...

I made dinner and took care of Max. When we went to bed, he had sex with me without even offering an apology. And I let him do it. I was just fulfilling my duty, that's all.

Christmas 1976

In the meantime, Jacques was laid off for three months from the company where he worked. Just before the holidays, he signed up for unemployment insurance. Since I was still working, we managed our budget well.

Natasha came to spend the holidays with us. I had five days off. She would spend New Year's Day with Mrs. Bélisle. It was our first Christmas as a family. We spoiled the children: they received many gifts from both of us, my brother and my sister Irène. As usual, she didn't come to the house, but she participated from afar. I called her, and I went to visit her with the children.

Jacques and my brother drank almost a gallon of wine. They had settled in the living room to drink. By the end of the evening, they tried to get up, but they couldn't stand on their feet and collapsed on the living room floor. I helped them get up and put them to bed. The next day, we laughed about the incident. The children were happy with their gifts and content. It was wonderful!

An Unexpected Event

One day, I received a check for thirty-five dollars from Tony, Max's father, supposedly for Max's child support. I didn't understand because, since our confrontation in court, I hadn't received a penny from him. I was confused and puzzled. I kept the check, but I never cashed it. I never received another one. My lawyer had wanted to make deductions from his salary, but I had refused. That's all there is to say about that story. It's Tony, who had decided to abandon his son, right?

Part Four

Buying Our First House

The idea of buying a house had never crossed our minds. Until one day, one of our friends, Paola, called to tell me she had bought a house in Terrebonne. She also invited me to visit her, suggesting we take the opportunity to check out a few model homes. "You never know, maybe you and your husband will find one you like," she added. I accepted her invitation and told her I would call her back for directions.

It was in 1978, shortly after the birth of my daughter, that I met Paola in an English class. Since then, we had remained friends. She lived in Terrebonne with her husband Simon and their three little girls.

One Sunday, I called her for directions. The appointment was set for 4:30 PM. To get to Saint-Louis-de-Terrebonne, we took Highway 25. The trip took 25 minutes. Our friends showed us their house and then explained the steps involved in buying our own. They offered to show us model homes. The sales office was still open. We looked at several models with the manager, who explained the different options available. The house we liked was a cottage with three bedrooms upstairs and one bathroom. On the ground floor, there was the living room, dining room, kitchen, a powder room, and the basement. The down payment was set at 1,000 dollars. It seemed interesting, but we told our contact that we would think it over and get back to him.

The house had not yet been built. We had simply chosen the location. All we had to do was give our approval, and the builder would start the work (subject to the acceptance of the mortgage loan).

Back home, we discussed the matter. Jacques thought we should first check if it was possible to find a house in Montreal at a better price. He mentioned cottages he had noticed on Saint-Zotique Street, in the east of the city.

We did go check them out. They were houses of the same style as the one we were interested in, but they were much more expensive, and the down payment was $5,000.

So, our choice was made: we decided on the house in Saint-Louis-de-Terrebonne. It was clearly more advantageous for our budget. However, Jacques told me that since he wasn't working, we didn't currently have the $1,000 (the down payment) available. I quickly reassured him by assuring him that I would find the necessary amount within two days.

The very next day, in Jacques' absence, I called my sister Irène, asking her for almost $1,000. Given her deep affection for me and my children, she immediately agreed. Then she told me, "I'm doing this for you and the children, not for Jacques." After thanking her, I called Jacques' employer, asking for an employment verification letter, acknowledging that my husband had been unemployed for more than a month. He first reviewed Jacques' file and then told me, "The work stoppage is indeed for two months; tell Jacques to come by tomorrow to pick up the letter." I thanked him wholeheartedly, silently praying to God to bless him.

Armed with these two positive responses, I informed Jacques that I would call the builder to finalize the details of the house purchase. "How are you going to manage, without money and without a letter of recommendation?" he asked. Fixing him seriously, I replied, "Tomorrow, you will go to get the recommendation letter from your supervisor — I had contacted him about this — and my sister has agreed to lend me the $1,000." Monsieur remained speechless. But not a word of thanks from him!

Thus, thanks to my perseverance and determination, I acquired my first house. Since I had a stable job, we didn't face any problems with the bank. The house was built, and two months later, we went to the notary. In February 1977, in the middle of winter, we moved in. This was after we had terminated our lease, and the landlord had asked us to pay a one-month penalty.

We had lived in this apartment on Baillargé Street for six months. Reflecting on my memories, I realized many things had happened there. Many of these events, or the anecdotes related to them, will, however, remain unknown to the reader, in order to let my secret garden bloom!

Chapter 5

Moving to Saint-Louis-de-Terrebonne (1976-1985)

First Part

Everything was ready for the move: friends to help us, food for lunch and dinner, vehicles for transportation, including the trailer, etc.

Jacques had attached the trailer to the back of my brother's car, which he drove, while I drove his, a Renault. It was winter, very cold, snowing, and the road was icy.

During the first trip, my friend and I stayed at the house in Saint-Louis-de-Terrebonne to do some dusting. We also placed the dishes and linens in the cupboards and prepared the meal.

Jacques and his companions first brought the stove and refrigerator so we could prepare food. They left with one of the older boys from my friend Nélia's family. I reminded Jacques to be cautious and drive carefully.

We had enough time to arrange everything and prepare lunch and dinner, and our guys were still not back. Fortunately, I had them eat a small snack before they left. For dinner, I had cooked fried pork with rice and red beans, and a nice salad. For drinks, there was juice, no beer, but just a little Barbancourt rum (from Haiti) to warm us from the cold. They finally returned around 4 PM. They explained, "We ran into a lot of problems on the highway with the trailer. The car was sliding on the ice." They were exhausted. Since they had brought all the heavy furniture, I told them, "For the little that remains, Jacques and I can continue tomorrow." We still had a few days before handing over the apartment key, and during those days, I planned to do a final cleaning in it.

I first made them eat, and then they warmed up with a small glass of rum. After that, they unloaded the furniture and carried it into the house. Before they left, almost everything was in place. Jacques and I then returned to Montreal to bring everyone back. I took the opportunity to clean the apartment and retrieve mechanical and DIY tools that belonged to Jacques.

We went to meet the friends who lived upstairs to thank them and say goodbye. Then, we left to start our new life as homeowners.

Second Part

Description of the Saint-Louis-de-Terrebonne House and Neighborhood

The house was located at the corner of Terrasse des Princes Street and Boulevard des Seigneurs. There was a small park named Terrasse des Princes in the center of the street, surrounded by houses similar to ours, which is where the name Terrasse des Princes came from. They were all newly built houses, most of the owners had moved in at the same time. My house was a family unit, a cottage. The backyard overlooked an empty lot: no fence, no garage. Nothing had been set up yet. The land was covered in snow. There were three bedrooms and a bathroom upstairs, with a half-bath downstairs. The living room was very large, with a fireplace. The entrance faced the stairs to the upper floor. To the right of the hallway was the living room, to the left was the half-bath and laundry area. Immediately after, there was the kitchen and dining room. From the patio door and the kitchen window, you could see the backyards of the other houses, Terrasse des Princes street, and Boulevard des Seigneurs. From the kitchen window, while preparing meals, I could keep an eye on the children playing outside and observe the flow of passersby on both streets. The basement, which was concrete and half-insulated, was unfinished. We still had quite a bit of work to do. The main thing, however, was that we were living in our own house.

Jacques, on the other hand, was already imagining what he would do with the basement and the lot. And I could see it coming!

Saint-Louis-de-Terrebonne was located 25 minutes from Montreal by car and two and a half hours by bus, considering the stops and schedule. As it was a new residential area, we had to go to another small village, 35 minutes away from Saint-Louis-de-Terrebonne, to collect our mail. The school was still under construction, so we had to temporarily enroll Max in the school of the neighboring village. On Sundays, we attended church at Vieux-Terrebonne. All these inconveniences made our beginnings quite difficult.

But gradually, things started to fall into place. Once the school was completed, my son could walk there. And every Sunday, we celebrated mass there.

Then, Canada Post installed mailboxes at the corner of each street. A CLSC was built near us, and a clinic opened on Boulevard des Seigneurs in Terrebonne. At first, we shopped at a commercial center in Terrebonne, but later, a small shopping center was built in Saint-Louis-de-Terrebonne. At the corner of Boulevard des Seigneurs and a few other streets was a bakery, the owner of which was one of our neighbors. I could walk to the small shopping center, especially to buy fresh, hot bread.

Third Part

Our Start in Saint-Louis-de-Terrebonne

On the night of our first night in the house, I went to bed before Jacques. He was in the process of placing his tools and other items in the basement. When he came up to bed, he woke me up by whispering, "You shouldn't be asleep already, we need to baptize the house. Hurry up! Wake up! I need to have a good fuck tonight. I'm tired, but it will do me good. We're alone in this big house, you can scream as much as you want. No one will hear you. I'll take you as I want, and how I want." At that moment, he usually grits his teeth and moans, "Hold on, Enice!"

I tried to explain that I was feeling tired and that we could take our time. "No way," he shouted, "Come here!"

It was the first time I had seen him so aggressive. He really scared me. I tried to reassure myself, telling myself that his attitude was temporary, that he was simply tired. In fact, I felt deeply disturbed. I let him do what he wanted. As usual, he fell asleep immediately after relieving himself, and I went to the bathroom to wash myself with hot water to ease the pain, since my vagina had become very sensitive. I barely slept. I did not like what he had done. The next day, I said nothing to him, otherwise, he would have hurt me even more.

I had a dream during the little sleep I managed to get. It was the first time I saw the unknown lover in my dreams (a character from my first book, {*Tales of a Multifaceted Life*). In my dream, I was in my house in Saint-Louis-de-Terrebonne; I heard a knock at the door, went to open it, and to my great surprise, it was him. Without saying a word, he smiled at me and entered the vestibule. He looked at himself in the mirror I had placed on the wall in the entrance. He touched it to fix it. He looked at the rooms on the ground floor from both sides and climbed the stairs to the upper floor; he looked at the bedrooms. After a pause, he whispered to me, his eyes filled with love: "I will always be here for you," and gently caressed my face before leaving.

I felt a sense of peace and fulfillment, something I had only felt when we were lovers in New York. The next morning, upon waking, I felt recharged by the dream. I didn't tell anyone about my dream. It was my little secret, something that would help me cope with the challenges I would face, without me realizing it.

It was Sunday. We went to pick up Max from his caretaker, Mrs. Bélisle. We didn't stay long because we still needed to arrange things in the house. Since I had another day off on Monday, I went to enroll Max in his new school and took the opportunity to inquire about the school transportation options.

Jacques had not yet resumed work. In the morning, he would drive me to mine around seven o'clock. In the afternoon, he would pick Max up from school and then come to get me from work. I had to wait an hour for him. It was a temporary situation since we were discussing the possibility of buying a second car.

Meanwhile, Jacques had started remodeling the basement. He planned to install wooden flooring, insulation, and plumbing for the future construction of a kitchen. I helped him put the drywall on the ceiling. Jacques had the bad habit of turning the music volume up to an exaggerated level, to the point where we could barely hear each other. He worked every day, even on the weekends. One time when Jacques was cooking soft-boiled eggs, he forgot about them, and Max, noticing that they were about to burst, immediately called his father, who came to extinguish the fire. I then decided that he shouldn't prepare meals anymore, as it was becoming dangerous.

Eventually, we decided to give Max a key in case no one was home when he returned from school. The key was placed on a cord around his neck, and we made it clear to him never to give the key to anyone or open the door to anyone. Max was naturally a bit rebellious, but as he grew older, he became very receptive when it came to security. We also advised him to go to our neighbor's house in case of an emergency. Of course, we informed our neighbor about this.

One day, when I was at work and Max was at school, Jacques, who was still working on the house, decided to prepare dinner, rice with beans. He then forgot to turn off the stove, leaving the pot on it. He was supposed to pick up my brother Robert and then come get me from work. That evening, a strong snowstorm delayed us on the highway. When we arrived, Jacques had to spend a long time clearing the driveway due to the heavy snow accumulation. On my side, not seeing Max anywhere, I began to worry. Suddenly, he came from the neighbor's house, explaining proudly: "I came back with my friend Jean (the neighbor's son). I went to his place when I noticed the house was empty and I couldn't get in."

Upon entering the house, one of the stove burners had been left on with a pot covering it, ready to explode. I immediately reacted, urging my brother to open the patio door, grabbed the pot without removing the lid, and threw it into the snow. It exploded like a small bomb. I then turned off the stove and shouted, "Thank you, Jesus and Mother Marie Rose." When we had moved into the house, I had placed a picture of Mother Marie Rose on the kitchen wall next to the fan. I had prayed to her, asking her to protect my house from fires. I wanted to express my gratitude to her.

Mother Marie Rose is the founder of the Congregation of the Sisters of Saint Name of Jesus and Mary in Montreal, on Mont-Royal Street.

Fourth Part

The Disadvantages — Financial Difficulties

We continued to live our lives quietly. The many round trips, the cold, and the snow that never seemed to end. Our possession of the house hadn't cost us much, but since Jacques had not yet returned to work and our expenses had increased, money started becoming scarce. At that time, we didn't have credit cards. Our purchases were made with cash. At one point, I had caught a bronchitis, and the doctor had prescribed antibiotics. Well, I couldn't buy them because I didn't have enough money. I was waiting for my paycheck. I had to call my sister who lived in Montreal. I then suggested to Jacques that he call his employer to see if he could return to work. Since he couldn't decide to do so, I decided to call Mr. Bertrand (the director) myself. On his suggestion, I asked Jacques to contact his supervisor after lunchtime, which he did.

The supervisor then offered Jacques to start working at night, that same day (from midnight to seven in the morning). We were very happy. But after that, the situation became a bit complicated: I had to drive Jacques to work at night, then return home to sleep a bit; then I had to go back to pick him up at 7 a.m., so he could drop me off at my work at 7:30 a.m. Afterward, he quickly took Max to his school for 8:30 a.m. Max would continue sleeping soundly in the car until arriving at school. At midnight, when I went to pick up Jacques, I took Max with me. We had to settle for this inconvenient arrangement for quite some time.

I had to get up at 4:30 a.m. to prepare the lunches, breakfast, etc., and then leave for work at 6:30 a.m. And as for the sexual relations, it was painful! He was never satisfied. He needed it constantly; before going to work at night, upon his return just before sleeping, during the holidays... It was: "Enice, hold the position," with no affection.

Life went on, spring arrived, the snow began to slowly melt, and the temperature became milder. Mrs. Bélisle, Natasha's caretaker, informed us that she could no longer take care of Natasha because her health was declining. We would have to think about taking Natasha with us. She gave us a grace period to find a new caretaker. Since there was a daycare very close to my workplace on Vincent D'Indy Street, I went to enroll Natasha. I considered myself lucky as there was still space available.

The daycare hours were from 7 a.m. to 5 p.m. That worked well for me; I would have enough time to get to work by 7:30 a.m. Jacques had applied for a job either during the day or at night. He was able to get the night job. This was an improvement because he could drop me off at work in the morning. In the afternoon, after work, I would pick Natasha up from the daycare, and we would take the bus back to Saint-Louis-de-Terrebonne. Max was waiting quietly at the neighbor's house. But for me, it was hell. I would arrive home after 8 p.m. I had to prepare dinner, help Max with his homework, give the children their baths, put them to bed, and prepare the lunches for the next day. By the time I finished everything, it was already past midnight. And just when I was about to go to bed, Jacques would come in after having eaten his meal; he would want to make love. The next day, I had to get up at 4 a.m. again to prepare breakfast, finish the lunches, and get the kids ready. We had to leave early because of the traffic.

It had become intolerable. I warned Jacques that if we didn't buy another car, I wouldn't last much longer. He agreed and suggested we buy a used car. A week later, I got a small Austin car from the classifieds. It was white.

It was my first experience with a car with a manual transmission; I learned to drive it in a week. At the beginning of my learning process, Jacques used it to go to work, and I drove his Toyota. It was better for everyone. The family spent more time together, and it was less exhausting for the children.

Fifth Part

The Neighbors — The Outdoor Layout

The new homeowners began to settle in the neighborhood. We had Haitian neighbors, and across the street at the corner of Terrasse des Princes, another family moved in. A little further down, two other Haitian families, along with several others from different ethnic backgrounds. Almost all of them had children.

Our closest neighbor, Marianne, had a five-year-old son, about the same age as Natasha. Marianne's mother looked after both of her little boys at home. When we first started socializing with her, she made an offer to us. She suggested that her mother could take care of our children, especially Natasha. This way, Natasha wouldn't have to travel every day. We told her we'd think about it. After much reflection, particularly on my part with feelings of fear and doubt, we decided to accept. But my concern still lingered.

One day, while I was at work, one of my patients, Sister Margherita, noticed and said, "My dear, for the past few days, I've noticed you've been pensive; you're in the clouds, though you try to hide it. I know you well, and I want you to tell me what's going on." I shared with her that I had entrusted the care of my children to strangers, and it troubled me. She reassured me, saying, "Don't worry. There are angels watching over them. You're so kind and gentle with us, I don't think anything will happen to your children. Pray to God, ask him to protect them, and I will also pray for them." Miraculously, I stopped worrying so much. After work, I hurried to get home early. The lady only looked after the children in the afternoons, from 2:00 to 4:30 p.m., just until I got back.

With the daycare problem solved, the atmosphere at home became less tense. Until then, I had never taken the time to think about my own well-being. I focused all my attention on Jacques, the children, and my household duties. Just thinking about all of this makes me sad. I took care of everyone in case they got sick. But for me, no one took care of me. The children couldn't, they were too young, and as for Jacques, I avoided telling him I was sick because then he would complain, saying, "I've spent my life hearing my mother say: I'm sick! I'm sick? I wouldn't want a wife who complains all the time that she's sick." I said nothing and didn't reveal my health condition to anyone; I took my medicine to get better.

We started to get to know a few neighbors, and the children made friends, especially Max, since Natasha was still too young. It was the time of the snowmelt; spring was almost over, and summer was just beginning.

Our neighbors started preparing their plots for lawn installation and outdoor layouts, such as small gardens, sheds, and fences. Almost everyone hired a contractor to do the work. Jacques, on the other hand, decided to do everything himself. I advised him to have someone else build at least the fence, but he categorically refused. "It's not too difficult," he argued, "I can do it myself." In addition to building the fence, the land needed to be tilled to plant the grass. When Jacques began digging holes for the fence posts, the operation turned out to be very difficult because many large stones were buried in the ground. My brother Robert, my nephew Riva, and some friends came to help us. My nephew Riva, who lived with my sister Irène, had come from Haiti to study electronic engineering.

Thanks to their extreme determination, they managed to put up the fence, level the ground, and apply fertilizer and seed. Jacques succeeded in growing grass over the entire yard, while I planted flowers and trees in the front, including a maple tree that I wanted to place in the middle of the yard and two fir trees on each side of the large window.

Now, when I pass in front of that house, I find it beautiful with its lovely trees and flowers. We had placed a large stone in the middle of the front yard. Every person who visited us had their photo taken sitting on the large stone. I made a vegetable garden in the yard. I managed to harvest corn, lettuce, carrots, and tomatoes.

Jacques built a shed and a deck in the yard one weekend, just next to the house, near the fence. Two days later, he received a letter from the city stating that he was not allowed to build the shed there, and that he had to demolish it and rebuild it at the back of the house. Jacques wasn't too happy; he seemed even discouraged. He had ten days to comply. "The land is mine," he protested, "I can do whatever I want with it." I reminded him that he had to follow the law. He took down the shed and rebuilt it at the back according to the permitted dimensions.

As for the deck, it was redone at least four or five times during the years we lived in that house.

A Reflection

Looking back at the past, I sometimes wonder if it wasn't by dismantling and rebuilding that Jacques developed a habit of tearing everything down in every house we purchased afterward. It became an obsession: he would dismantle the interior of each new house to rebuild it. We always lived in what felt like a construction site because it would take months or even years to complete the renovations. In fact, it was almost always at the time of selling the houses that he decided to finish the renovations.

Since it was summer and I was feeling well, I did my best not to upset him. I took care of everything in the house. Jacques, on the other hand, took care of the mechanical maintenance of the cars and the house renovations. Occasionally, I would give him a hand. I was exhausted; the children, of course, couldn't help me, they were too young. Gradually, I began showing them how to make their beds and put some order in their rooms.

Sixth Part

The Neighbors and the Environment

Some of our neighbors became friends with us. Our closest neighbors, Marianne and her husband Richard, had two children, one two years old and the other four. The older one was very rambunctious. The husband took pleasure in beating his wife. Realizing that I felt pity for her, Marianne confided in me, "You haven't seen anything yet, it's his habit. When we lived in Montreal, he once hurt me on the head. The police came. Don't worry about me!"

It is a fact that abused women carry very painful wounds, often very visible! But I think the psychological wound is even more terrible; it kills slowly and sometimes leads to madness or death.

As of the latest news, this couple (still together) moved to live in Miami, Florida. I had also become friends with the neighbors across the street, especially with the woman, Fanny. She also had two boys, one five years old and the other two. She did sewing for individuals and manufacturers. She worked a lot. Her children became friends with mine. This family, too, eventually moved away. We also socialized with another family: Gustave, the husband, worked as a taxi driver, while the wife worked in a factory. Their daughter, Darla, was almost the same age as mine, and they also had a son. Darla was my daughter's favorite friend.

They were always together with a little Italian boy named Gino. The three were inseparable. Gino had an older brother. Their parents were not our friends, but I occasionally spoke with the mother. Many other families lived in the village. Almost all of these people have left Saint-Louis-de-Terrebonne.

My neighborhood had many children. Édouard, Max's little friend whose house was behind ours, would ring our doorbell as early as 6 a.m. to ask to see Max. "It's vacation time," I would explain, "Max doesn't wake up early." I would watch him from the window: he would sit on the steps of our porch, waiting for Max.

When I asked Max why Édouard didn't wait for him at his house, Max told me that every morning, his mother would send him out of the house and tell him, "Come back for lunch." After lunch, she would send him out again. If he wanted to drink some water, they would hand him a cup through the door. It was pitiful. Since the basement was almost finished, we had set up a television and toys for the children. From that day on, whenever he rang the bell, I would send him downstairs to wait until Max woke up. He was satisfied, and he didn't disturb anyone. I found it completely unacceptable for a mother to treat her child this way. She treated him like a little dog. Fortunately, she only had one child.

When my neighbor Marianne and her family moved out, an older couple than us bought their house. This couple had four older children: two were teenagers and the other two were a bit younger. One of the younger ones, a boy named Sony, was the same age as Max, and they became friends. His parents had installed an in-ground pool in their yard. It was a very nice Quebecois family. I wouldn't say we were really friends, but we would occasionally talk about things.

And our nurse friend who had advised me to buy the house had three daughters. The two twins were the same age as mine. She lived just three minutes' walk from our house. After an unfortunate incident, she moved to Montreal with her daughters.

On Jacques' advice, his colleague and friend Lucien, along with his wife Caroline, decided to buy a house in Saint-Louis-de-Terrebonne. The couple had five children. They lived almost ten minutes from our house. They were the last to arrive. To this day, they still live in Saint-Louis-de-Terrebonne.

At our children's birthdays, it was always grand… With only the neighborhood friends, we gathered over twenty children. Natatsha's birthday was in July; during the summer, we could celebrate outside and have even more fun. The children loved my homemade pizzas, my homemade little pies, and especially the cake. They had so much fun, especially after we installed an above-ground pool in the yard. They would always come over when I was on vacation because Jacques didn't want to supervise them. For me, on the other hand, it was wonderful times.

I really love children, not just my own, but all children. In my view, a child should always be happy. It is at this stage in their lives, before adulthood, that they must fully enjoy their life. A child without love is an unhappy child. It is up to us, the adults, to assist them while providing a good education and the necessary guidance, always in a climate of love. Because they are the extension of our lives and our hopes.

Seventh Part

The Basement Layout — The School

The summer vacation over, the children went to their new school in Saint-Louis-de-Terrebonne, located at the top of the hill. They walked there.

Max was in third grade, and Natatsha was in pre-kindergarten. At the parent-teacher meeting, we learned that Max had a bad report card. Since his birthday, November 6th, was approaching, Jacques decided to punish him. This was how: "For your birthday, you won't get any presents from anyone. In fact, I'm going to call all our friends to let them know that I don't want any presents for Max, because he didn't get a good report." I tried to calm Jacques down: "With all these changes, he's having trouble adjusting. We'll give him a smaller gift." He replied, "No, otherwise he'll get a bad report card again at Christmas."

Of course, on his birthday, Max was not celebrated, and he didn't receive any presents. It was cruel for a seven-year-old child. Jacques only built a small wooden truck like the ones made in Haiti. I made a cake that we cut as a family, and that was it. It was obvious that I felt much more pain than he did. In any case, it wasn't easy to know what was going on in this little child's heart.

At Christmas, Max got a good report card. I bought him several beautiful gifts. My sister also generously rewarded him.

Jacques finished the basement during the winter. I helped him as much as I could. He built a closed bedroom, a small open kitchen, a bar, and a playroom.

We moved the dining room downstairs, and later we bought another one with a china cabinet for the main floor. Jacques painted the basement floor, after which we installed a wood stove in the playroom and a recirculation fan that spread the heat to the top floor. In the evening, the whole family would settle in the basement, the children to do their homework, Jacques to tinker while watching television. Once the basement was finished, I had less cleaning to do.

Later, we decided to change the paint color — it had been painted white — and to wallpaper the whole house, except for the kitchen and the children's rooms, due to allergy risks. I chose eggshell color for the living room, hallway, and kitchen, peach for my room, pink for Natatsha, and blue for Max. For the back wall of the dining room, a wallpaper depicting an autumn forest. Beige ceramic tiles with small patterns for the kitchen wall and light brown ceramic tiles with beige patterns for the entrance.

We did all the work ourselves. I chose the wallpaper and the dining room furniture. After all these renovations, the house was radiant, spotless, and very inviting. I felt a sense of well-being every time I came home.

The children had become calmer. Jacques, on the other hand, was always looking for something to do. It was like an illness. The fact that he continued to control the family budget didn't really bother me, as I hadn't yet taken the time to examine the validity of such an arrangement. I was dealing with too many things at once: the children's education, as well as their extracurricular activities. Jacques wasn't interested in accompanying them. I felt more and more exhausted, while he became more and more demanding. In fact, he was primarily thinking about himself, and his words confirmed this without any ambiguity.

The Arrival of Aunt Dieula in Montreal

During the summer holidays, Aunt Dieula, who lived in Haiti, came to spend three months in Montreal at my sister's and my place. She arrived in August when the temperature was starting to cool down, which she didn't like. "How do people live in a country like this?" she complained. "There's almost no one in the streets, no one comes for coffee. And you're always working and taking care of the children when you're home. This isn't a life. I'm much better off at home."

I took the time to explain to her that life is always like this in a foreign country. She was always cold, even though it was still summer. I still remember the following anecdote about Aunt Dieula. One day, before I left for work, we gave her this recommendation: "Aunt Dieula, if you go outside, dress warmly; never wash yourself with cold water." She replied, "I, Dieula, François, have always washed myself with cold water; no one will change my habits." I advised her to still be very careful. Unfortunately, she ignored our warnings and washed herself with cold water. Later, she admitted that she had thought she might die, so cold she had been. She got into bed and buried herself under several blankets to warm up. A little later, noticing that it was sunny on the terrace at the back of the house, she decided to go out to warm up. No jacket, despite the children's warnings. After ten minutes, she came back inside because she was still cold. I made her drink some warm rum. Since she ached all over, we set up a heating massage device in her bed, and she hated the experience and wanted to return immediately to Haiti. However, she still had a month left to stay in Montreal. She caused us a lot of worries. In the end, she left very happy with her stay. Back in Haiti, she told everyone who would listen: "I went to the land of the Whites, I'm a big lady now."

Eighth Part

My Divorce from Tony in 1979

Since I was living with Jacques, the legal aid office informed me that I needed to find another lawyer to continue the divorce proceedings. Together, we made enough money to afford a lawyer's services. From a list, I chose one, informing him that I wanted the divorce as quickly as possible. After reviewing my case, he promised he would do everything he could to satisfy me. A few months later, he informed me that the hearing would take place at the Saint-Jérôme courthouse, and that Tony would be present.

On the day of the hearing, after questioning me about the cause of my divorce request, the judge was surprised by Tony's absence. My lawyer was also unaware of the reason. The judge reviewed the case and pronounced the divorce. This chapter of my life was definitively closed and put away once and for all.

I had repeatedly told Jacques that if he didn't ask me to marry him, he shouldn't expect me to do it for him. He would always repeat that marriage wasn't necessary; that if he got married, it would just be for a piece of paper, that's all. In fact, there were other reasons: we wanted Natatsha, his daughter, to carry his name; he also wanted to proceed with adopting both children. We no longer had a choice.

One day, Jacques decided to talk to me about marriage. He said, "Enice, you should pick a date for next summer for the wedding; then we'll go buy the rings, my suit, and your wedding dress at the same time." "Is that how you're proposing?" I said. He replied, "If you don't want to, just tell me." I told him I would choose a date.

All of this, without any romance, that's how things went between us. And I ended up behaving like him. With Jacques, everything happened in bed. I began losing the last affectionate feelings I had for him.

Ninth Part

The Penances

I became pregnant; after two months, I lost the baby because I was too tired; my hemoglobin levels had significantly dropped.

Life went on... the children were growing fast. I did a deep cleaning of the entire house twice a month. I had the children help me. They liked it, especially Natatsha, who was slim and appeared quite tall for her age. I called her "my little chip." When she became older, she told me one day, “Mammy, I don’t like it when you call me ‘my little chip.’” I explained that it was because I loved her. She replied, “No, I don’t like it.” I respected her decision. I started calling her only by her first name, Natatsha; she was happy with that. Max had a nickname, Bitou. It was my brother Robert who had given it to him when he was a baby. I noticed that every time I called him that when his friends were at our place, he didn’t react negatively and would show a subtle smile.

One day, his sister told me, “Mammy, Max doesn’t like being called Bitou. You should tell people not to call him that.” I simply said, “Oh, really.” She added, “Yes, that’s how it is.” Since then, I stopped calling him that. I used his first name, Max.

At eight years old, Max was already mowing the lawn. It was like a game for him. He also took out the trash. Once, he forgot to do it, and Jacques went and emptied the trash bag in his room. I begged him not to do it. “That way,” he argued, “Max will never forget to do it again.” I think it was after this scene that Natatsha and I made a schedule for Max and stuck it on the wall of his room to help him remember the garbage collection days.

Jacques gave strange punishments to the children. One time, Max had left his room a bit messy. Hearing a noise upstairs, I went up, followed by Natatsha. When we arrived, we froze, mouths agape. Jacques had ransacked the room. The mattress was on the floor, the drawers overturned on the bed frame, Max's clothes on the floor, etc. It was a disaster, and Jacques found it funny, laughing about it.

I felt sorry for Max. My daughter sighed, "My poor brother." After turning my son's room upside down, Jacques dropped, "He'll have work to do when he gets back from basketball; it will teach him a lesson." As I write this part of my life, tears well up in my eyes.

I was not at all happy. I spoke to Jacques in a calm voice, saying, "You know, you shouldn't do this to Max." My remark irritated him even more: "You're the one spoiling the children!" he yelled. "Max is mommy's little boy. All I did was correct him. And I don't want to hear anything or see you comforting the children when I punish them." I said nothing more. I cried. When my son arrived, he was shocked. He didn't cry, but his eyes were filled with tears. I gave him a small caress, then Natatsha and I helped him put his room back in order. Jacques, meanwhile, stayed downstairs. When I went down, he threw nonsense at me, roaring, "You spoil the children, you're always kissing them, coddling them."

I remained silent. I finished my housework. He went upstairs to bed, announcing that he was waiting for me in the bedroom. I took my time; I was ashamed of him.

It is true that Max was a bit mischievous; like most children his age, he liked to have fun. Max might also have been burdened with too many responsibilities. For example, in addition to going to school and participating in extracurricular activities, he had to help Jacques renovate the house, take out the trash, mow the lawn, shovel snow, etc. At times, he let off steam with his toys. He never hurt any of his friends, he never refused any of our requests. He was a very intelligent boy, as all his teachers confirmed, but often he acted in a way that sought attention.

As a teenager, he liked to apply gel to his hair and was very interested in beauty products. One time, we went to a parent-teacher meeting when Max was in 2nd grade, and his French and History teachers pointed out that Max would achieve better academic results if he didn't go to the bathroom so often to fix his hair. They advised us to talk to him about it. On the way home, Jacques stayed silent. When he behaved like this, it was a very bad sign. I then took the risk of asking, "Jacques, what are you thinking?" He replied that he had a little idea! When we arrived in the house's parking lot, I saw Max watching us from the window. He had the expression of a little child devastated by fear.

I suggested to Jacques that we should just talk to him sternly. He replied, "I have news for you." I said, "What?" With clenched teeth, he announced to me: "I'm going to shave his hair completely." I groaned, "Oh, no!" Not that! He replied, "Oh, yes!" while snickering. It was really hellish. I didn't know what to do to stop him from carrying out his threat. I begged him, but his mind was already made up. I was so worried for my son. Max knew the news wasn't good, but he would have never thought his father would commit such a cruel act.

He was sitting docilely in the corner of the sofa. Jacques took a razor and a chair, and he said to Max: "Come sit here, my little man; I'm going to shave your hair down to the skin." His sister had her hands on her jaw, her mouth open, and her eyes filled with tears. On my side, I felt that my heart was going to stop beating.

On my side, I felt like my heart was going to stop beating. Max looked dazed and teary-eyed.

Max looked dazed and his eyes were watery. His work done, Jacques ordered Max to clean the floor and forbade me from helping him. But I didn't listen to him and helped my son. Hoping to comfort him, I whispered to him: "You know, Max, you'll do better next time, okay!" Please, do it for yourself and for mom. After cleaning, I went upstairs with the children to put them to bed. Max and his sister stayed in one of the rooms to talk; I don't know what they talked about. I then went downstairs to talk with Jacques. Before going to bed, I went to see Max; he was sleeping deeply, but his body was moving. It looked like he was having a nightmare. I gave him a little kiss, and he calmed down.

I gave him a little kiss, and he calmed down. That night, I didn't want Jacques to touch me.

That night, I didn't want Jacques to touch me. I was too angry. "Do you want to avenge your beloved son?" he grumbled. Here, in this house, I'm the boss! Then, he got close to me; I didn't turn around. He then shook me and made me fall onto the floor. I simply took a sheet to lie down on the floor. Pressing myself with rage on the floor, he finally raped me. I didn't react; I was disgusted.

I didn't react, I felt disgust.

He inflicted very long punishments on Max. He could lock him in his room for a week. Max only came down to eat and go to the bathroom. My son was so afraid of Jacques that he endured those abusive punishments without protesting. One summer day, when the weather was nice and Jacques had put Max on punishment before leaving for work, I invited him to join us, Natasha and I, in front of the television. He refused. I insisted by promising him that, if anything happened with Jacques, I would defend him. But he didn't want to leave his room.

But he didn't want to leave his room. I think Max was affected by these events.

I believe that Max was deeply affected by these events. Today, he protects his own children by declaring that he doesn't want them to suffer as he did in his childhood. He doesn't raise his voice with them, he respects them, and he shows them a lot of affection. When I observe the way he interacts with his children, I start to think: "My God, what a good father he is!" One day, he confided to his sister: "I don't want my children to experience what I went through with my two fathers." I will always do everything I can to protect them. Looking back on the past, I realize how much this boy has suffered. This house in Saint-Louis-de-Terrebonne has been the scene of so many painful incidents! Max endured many more punishments than his sister Natasha, Jacques's daughter. Since she had a temperament very different from Max's, her father found it difficult to punish her: from a young age, she had taken her place and had managed to create her own means of defense. By observing the way Jacques interacted with his brother, she managed to gain the upper hand.

I still remember the first time Jacques imposed a punishment on Natatsha. She was six years old. One morning, she didn't want to go to school. She was already fully dressed, but she was complaining of a stomach ache. Her brother was waiting for her outside with friends. She said she was tired. I then asked her if she was sick, and she replied in the negative. I was off that day. It had become a habit for her: every time I was off work, Natatsha would make arrangements to stay with me at home. "You can stay home today," I conceded, "but you have to go tomorrow." Having heard me, Jacques rushed down the stairs shouting, "You have to go to school." Natatsha replied that she wouldn't go, while crying bitterly. In the meantime, the other children had left. I suggested to Jacques to let her be "for today," but he grabbed her by the back collar of her coat to lift her up. He looked her in the eyes at the same time and yelled while throwing her into the room: "If that's how it is, go to your room and stay there for the day." His daughter replied in the same tone: "Okay." And acting like an adult, she closed the door to her room. Her little cat, Minou, was meowing at her door, and she let him in. She felt good with her cat, who was her friend and confident.

She felt good with her cat, who was her friend and confident. Jacques seemed extremely taken aback by his daughter's reaction.

Jacques seemed extremely taken aback by his daughter's reaction. A little later in the day, he let slip: "This little girl has a bad temper!" Well, I'll tame her. It seems that punishments don't bother her.

It seems that punishments don't bother her. One day, I noticed that Natatsha had a burn on one of her fingers.

One day, I noticed that Natatsha had a burn on one of her fingers. I asked her the reason. She simply replied, "It was Dad who burned me with matches." It is clearly a criminal act that, I admit, I should have reported to the police. When I asked Jacques to explain the reason for his despicable act, he gave me this justification: "That's how you have to tame her, she needs to feel the pain to understand." I did it so she wouldn't do it again, because she'll remember it for the rest of her life.

She didn't get punished often by her father. She was mischievous, but logical in her behavior. She kept everything in her heart. She always carried a blanket, her nanny doll, and her cat with her. They were her treasures. When she did her homework, she always kept her cat sitting or lying on her desk.

When she was doing her homework, she always kept her cat sitting or lying on her desk. Once, I don't know what had happened in her little head, she punished her cat.

Once, I don't know what had happened in her little head, she punished her cat. I spent an entire day looking for him. I even asked Jacques if he had seen it, and he told me no. A little later, while I was busy doing laundry in the laundry room, I heard a noise in the dirty laundry basket. I opened it, and Minou was sitting there quite comfortably. She wasn't even meowing. She was waiting for her owner to come and get her. I asked Natatsha if she knew why and how Minou ended up in the laundry basket in the washroom. She explained to me that she wanted to punish him because he had done something she didn't like. I told her that she had acted wrongly, since Minou was an animal. It wasn't worth punishing him; she could have killed him and regretted it afterward. I added that we don't punish for just anything. She understood me.

She understood me. Now that she has her children, I notice that she communicates a lot with them.

Now that she has her children, I notice that she communicates a lot with them. She doesn't punish them, but reprimands them, especially Mikael, who often cries. Usually, after scolding them, she explains her reasons: "Mom loves you very much, but she has to scold you when you do something forbidden." God sent mommy and daddy to protect you. Then, she gives them big kisses and hugs.

Then, she gives them big kisses and hugs. What you reap is what you have sown.

What we reap is what we had sown. Jacques planned to sow vengeance in the hearts of my children, but he did not achieve his goal. When he tried to sow vengeance, I was always there to sow love. Today, my children and grandchildren are filled with love. I thank God for it.

Tenth Part

Christmas and New Year's Eve; the celebrations

I enjoyed hosting friends at my house in Saint-Louis-de-Terrebonne for special occasions. Once, I organized a party for New Year's Eve. Despite the distance, the guests came in large numbers. To me, Christmas is sacred. Normally, I celebrate it with my family: with my children, Jacques, and sometimes my sister and brother.

As I've already emphasized, Christmas at our house was magical. I made sure everything was perfect and joyful. The decorations, the gifts, the food, the order in the house, not forgetting the Christmas tree and the midnight Mass, I took care of everything. I wanted my family to be happy. When the people around me are happy, I am too.

I would warn Jacques: "Everything must go well, please." He would reply: "You know what you need to do to make sure things go well." The children found their father kind; but what they didn't know was that I had to obey him to the letter to achieve that result. The children received many gifts from us, as well as from my sister and my brother.

At the beginning of our life together, Jacques would give me a card and a gift for Christmas and my birthday. Gradually, he stopped giving them to me. I never knew why. Perhaps it was just to test my intentions and feelings. I would secretly cry to prevent the children from discovering the drama I was living. I didn't tell anyone because I felt ashamed. But above all, I didn't want this problem to spoil the Christmas celebrations.

Almost every year, my sister would invite us to her house for New Year's Day, to spend the afternoon and evening with her and my brother. She would prepare good food. On this occasion, we would talk about everything and nothing. The children enjoyed the toys my sister had given them.

That year, Jacques didn't speak much. When he realized we were happy being together, without even having time for dinner, he decided we had to leave. He then came up with a trivial excuse. Despite our pleas, his decision was final. So, with the children, I followed him. He didn't speak to me in the car. Back at home, the children and I went to bed with heavy hearts. He, however, was proud of his actions.

In bed, he took me by force, declaring that he wouldn't spend the first day of the year without his gift! When he was done, I cried in the dark, and I fell asleep.

A second time, my sister invited me again for New Year's Day. She asked me this question: "Do you think Jacques will let you come?" I answered in the affirmative.

I answered affirmatively. This time, everything was fine.

This time, everything was fine. But, at one point during the evening, he got up abruptly as usual and, in the manner of a regiment commander, he declared: "It's time we leave." My sister was very angry this time. I told Jacques that I was staying. "Stay, he said, but I'm leaving and I won't come back to get you; so, figure out how to get home." He left without saying goodbye to anyone. My sister tried to reassure me: "Enice, don't think about it, have fun with us and the kids." I'll find someone to take you home. At that time, the children were very young. Throughout the evening, I kept thinking about what would happen to me when I got home. I stopped talking, and my sister noticed that I was pensive and worried. She was worried: "Are you afraid he'll hit you?" She called one of her friends and asked him to drive us home that same night, because I was afraid to sleep at her place.

She called one of her friends and asked him to drive us home that same night because I was afraid to sleep at her place. On our return, he was already in bed.

Upon our return, he was already in bed. I put the kids to bed, and after getting ready, I went to bed myself. He told me that he thought I would be sleeping at my sister's. I informed him that a friend of my sister had come to drive us. He mumbled, "Good thing you came tonight, otherwise you would have eaten a whole one." I replied that he couldn't beat me. He didn't respond. As soon as I got into bed, he climbed on top of me and pressed down so hard that I couldn't move or breathe, and he raped me with extreme aggression.

As soon as I lay down in bed, he climbed on top of me and pressed down so hard that I couldn't move or breathe, and he raped me with extreme aggression. The next day, January 2nd, he woke me up to have sex.

The next day, January 2nd, he woke me up to make love. I refused. He then started threatening me. He wanted to beat me. I struggled and fled the room. I rushed down the stairs like a madwoman, in my nightgown; once in the kitchen, I opened the door of one of the cabinets. He had bought a set of knives. I chose the longest knife and went back up to the room. During all this time, he was calling me, shouting aggressively: "Enice, come here right now." He was holding a belt in his hands, and I had a knife in mine.

"You see this knife," I shouted, "if one day you beat me, on that day, I would kill you!" And I wouldn't hesitate to do it. So, don't provoke me. I come from a lineage that is not afraid of blood.

I come from a lineage that does not fear blood. I had fire in my eyes and rage in my voice.

I had fire in my eyes and rage in my voice. He tried to take the knife from my hands, but he couldn't do it. He got scared and left me alone. The children were already awake. They were watching their favorite shows in the basement. I don't know if they heard the exchanges.

I don't know if they heard the exchanges. Since that day, he hasn't threatened me anymore.

Since that day, he hasn't threatened me anymore. He couldn't hit me, but he found another way to hurt me. It was through repeated rapes, degrading sexual acts. And he made me suffer mentally. It was disgusting and repugnant. I can't find strong enough words to describe this situation of sexual slavery in which I was plunged.

I can't find strong enough words to describe this situation of sexual slavery I was plunged into. Once, he punched my intimate parts while pretending to caress me.

Once, he punched my intimate parts while pretending to caress me. He twisted and turned it, clearly trying to hurt me. "The next time, he muttered, you'll listen to me." Then, he put his hands over my mouth. I almost lost consciousness. He was sneering and clearly enjoying penetrating me with a lot of force and brutality, saying, "It's good, it's good," and he ejaculated with contempt and arrogance.

He sneered and clearly took pleasure in penetrating me with a lot of force and brutality, saying, "It's good, it's good," and he released his semen with contempt and arrogance. When he was done, he simply fell asleep, like a baby, while I cried.

When he was done, he simply fell asleep, like a baby, while I cried. I couldn't walk. I had to drag myself to the bathroom. I heard a knock on the door. It was one of the children asking if I was okay. I told him yes and ordered him to go back to bed. In the bathroom, sobbing profusely, while wondering why I was enduring all these humiliations. I realized that an imminent danger was lurking, but what to do?

On another occasion, he sodomized me, unexpectedly. He had planned his move well. When I realized it, I asked him if he was crazy. I remember that I couldn't even move. He threw me onto the floor while holding me tightly against him, and while he was committing this act of sexual brutality, he pressed his hand violently against my diaper, while I cried. In addition to the indignation I felt, I sensed in my body all the abomination of the act he had just committed.

In addition to the indignation I felt, I sensed in my body the full abjection of the act he had just committed. When he was done, he said that I was his wife, that he could do whatever he wanted with me, and he was blackmailing me by adding that if I left him, people would call me a "little whore who left her husband for another man."

When he was done, he said that I was his wife, that he could do whatever he wanted with me, he was blackmailing me by adding that if I left him, people would call me a "little whore who left her husband for another man": One would conclude that Tony was right. I don't know why I felt like a zombie. In my opinion, it was the most atrocious act that left me forever tainted. Only a barbaric being could inflict such treatment on his wife.

Only a barbaric being could inflict such treatment on his wife. Despite all the martyrdom I was enduring, many people said they found me beautiful and attractive.

Despite all the martyrdom I was living through, many people said they found me beautiful and attractive. But they had no idea that, in my being and in my flesh, I was unhappy and suffering terribly. I continued to work anyway, I took care of the house and handled everything, without saying a word. I felt obligated to maintain the same lifestyle because of the children.

I felt obligated to maintain the same lifestyle because of the children.

Reflection

Reflection: These memories awakened in me the remnants of suffering that had ravaged my married life.

These memories awakened in me layers of suffering that had ravaged my couple's life. I have pain in my intimate areas, and I am suddenly seized by a frenzy that causes a wave of heat all the way to my sex. I pull my hair, I bang my head against the wall, I thrash my legs like a small child in pain. And I cry, I scream! Fortunately, I am alone in the apartment. I roar: "Enice, how and why did you endure all this?" Why?

And life goes on

And life goes on... Jacques, too, continued to work and displayed a very good mood.

Jacques, too, continued to work and displayed a very good mood. For him, everything was fine, since he knew he could rape me at will. He had become a sadistic being, an unpredictable and dangerous character.

He had become a sadistic being, an unpredictable and dangerous character. Once, we threw a party at home, the night before New Year's Day.

Once, we threw a party at home on New Year's Eve. I was wearing a beautiful black dress with straps and a white shawl. During the evening, I took it off at times because of the heat.

During the evening, I would take it off at times because of the heat. Throughout the evening, Jacques didn't speak to me.

All evening, Jacques didn't speak to me. He would occasionally cast me threatening and disdainful looks, making me feel guilty for who knows what. I wondered if it was my imagination playing tricks on me or if I was a victim of an optical illusion.

I was wondering if it was my imagination playing tricks on me or if I was a victim of an optical illusion. I kept serving my guests and trying to stay in a good mood.

I kept serving my guests and trying to be in a good mood. Our friends left, and he opposed me cleaning up that same evening. The children were already in bed. He calls me from the room on the upper floor, I go up right away.

He calls me from the room on the upper floor, I go up immediately. Having joined him in the room, I am about to point out to him that it was quite a lovely evening!

Having joined him in the room, I am about to point out to him that it was quite a lovely evening! But, at the same moment, he pulls me to him. He pulls me to him, tightening his grip around my waist, and sternly announces, "I'm going to tear this dress you wore tonight to shreds, so you won't go out in public dressed like a whore anymore." "Look closely!" And he starts tearing the dress by ripping off the straps. Having released me, he grabs a pair of scissors and continues to cut the dress into small pieces. I beg him to stop, but, as usual, in vain!

I beg him to stop, but, as usual, in vain! After completing his act of destruction, he savagely raped me.

His act of destruction complete, he savagely raped me. I believe the children heard everything. The next day, they asked me if I was feeling okay, with sorrow in their eyes. I tried to reassure them by whispering, not to worry about me, that everything was fine...

A ball by the Miragoânais Association of Montreal (June 24)

It seems that your message is empty. Could you please provide the text you would like me to translate?
We never attended the grand balls organized by the Haitians of Montreal because he didn't value that type of event. But we attended family parties and dance evenings organized by the Miragoânais association. I always made sure not to dance with another man out of fear of his reaction when we got home.

I always made sure not to dance with another man for fear of his reaction when we got home. It was at one of those Miragoan Association balls that I had seen my friend again.

It was at one of those balls of the Miragoan Association that I had seen my friend again. I felt very moved by his presence, but I didn't let it show. I was watching him from afar. I was strolling on the dance floor and there he was, right in front of me. He asked me if I was okay. I answered him affirmatively. He continued by confiding that he still thought about me, and I pointed out that it was the same on my side. Without ulterior motives.

Without ulterior motives. The rest of the evening went off without a hitch.

The rest of the evening went by without incident. Jacques didn't make any comments, since he had clearly noticed that the other person hadn't come back to talk to me.

Reflection

Enduring so many affronts and degrading treatments in order to provide those I love with the assurance of a stable family environment reveals a total abandonment of oneself. It is the sacrifice I unconsciously accepted to surround my two children with as much love as I could, even though, deep down, they suffered as much as I did.

By swallowing my sorrows and tears, I made it my mission to present them with a positive image of married life, which, I hope, will open the path to true love with their spouses and children.

Present Moment

Quebec, October 16, 2006

I am in Quebec to continue the journey of my past

It is 7 p.m. I am in Quebec, in the room of a retirement home at the Federation of Augustinian Monasteries. I settle in to write. I want to explain the preparation for my departure to Quebec, my arrival, and the atmosphere of the place. And also the reason why I temporarily stopped writing.

On New Year's Day 2006, I went to church, prayed, and meditated. I made the resolution to write in a neutral and quiet place.

After returning from New York, I stopped writing on October 18, 2004, due to a psychological block. I tried everything to continue; I even consulted a psychologist, but to no avail. I thought about it all the time and became more nervous. The fear of a permanent block haunted me: "My God, I implored, when will I have the strength to continue my story?"

The answer was obvious, but I didn't want to face it. I was afraid to continue; I felt very shaken, and perhaps a lack of self-confidence held me back.

To feel better, to regain my strength, and to find some spiritual peace, I decided to change my way of life. First, I enrolled at the sports center across from my house. I took daily walks and did stretching exercises. I took tai-chi and yoga classes. I also changed my eating habits and way of thinking. I finally decided to take control of my life and move forward without fear.

My daughter watched me without my knowledge. One day, she revealed to me that she found me different. She couldn't define exactly what had changed, but she felt I had become mentally a different person. I didn't confirm anything about it. I just told her I would be away for two weeks for a writing period in a retreat house in Quebec, at the Augustinian Monastery; I had booked from October 16 to 29. She completely approved of my decision; she didn't ask me a single question. She just promised that she would help with the accommodation expenses. I thanked her.

My arrival in Quebec and the atmosphere of the place.

I arrived at the Quebec terminal on October 16, 2006, at 3:45 p.m. I took a taxi to the retirement home of the Federation of Augustinian Monasteries. As soon as the driver dropped me off in front of the house, I thought, "This is the place I wanted to finish writing my manuscript. God has given it to me. I thank Him, and I must also thank my sister Irène, because it was she who recommended this place to me. She had come here during the summer with one of her friends for a short stay and had really enjoyed it."

After I registered, I received a paper from the secretary with my room number, 334, and a few instructions. I took the elevator and went up with my luggage.

Upon reaching the floor, as I walked down the corridor, I noted where the toilets and showers were. What I saw when I entered the room was beautiful. Through the window, I could see the river. I could also admire the large green space, the trees with their golden autumn leaves, paved paths for pedestrians, and so on. I was amazed by this harmony surrounding me.

I immediately went to the window to admire this wonderful gift that God had given me. Only after that did I observe the comfort and modesty of the room. It was a small room with a bed facing the window, a small desk, a chair, a rocking chair, a small bookshelf, a small sink, a medicine cabinet, a large wardrobe with shelves, and a closet. The room was clean and tidy. It was a perfect place for a retreat.

In the wardrobe, there were wool blankets, extra pillows, and a cabinet in the hallway. I took some extra pillows from the wardrobe to make sleeping more comfortable.

After placing my belongings in the wardrobe and desk drawers, I decided to explore the premises. Around 4:55 p.m., I went to the chapel before heading to dinner at 5:10 p.m. I stayed for 15 minutes. Upon feeling the atmosphere there, I was even more amazed. I felt an inexplicable peace and profound joy. I was moved, captivated. I knelt down and whispered, "My God, how well I feel! Thank you for everything." I couldn't say anything else; I just let myself be carried away by this gentle sensation that filled me. I closed my eyes to clear my mind, and I felt at peace. If I didn't have dinner, I would have stayed longer.

I promised myself that after dinner, I would explore the rest of the monastery and take a walk outside.

When I arrived at the cafeteria, I noticed that the nuns were eating. Hesitant to move forward, I stopped at the entrance. One of the nuns then came to get me. She asked if I was staying here for the first time, which I confirmed. "Come in," she said, "you are welcome." Then, she gently suggested that I take a tray and serve myself.

Dinner consisted of the main course and three dessert choices. The main dish was turkey in sauce with mashed potatoes. There were also broccoli, stuffed cauliflower with a white sauce, soup, and salad. Among the three dessert options, I chose a fruit cocktail. For a drink, I had a verbena and orange herbal tea. After a satisfying meal, I went back to my room to get a coat, intending to take a short walk outside (it was still quite chilly).

I walked for half an hour. Upon returning, I tried calling my daughter, but I couldn't reach her. I wanted to confirm that I had arrived at the monastery and that everything was fine. I then called my sister, and we talked for five minutes.

It is now 8:30 p.m.; I will stop writing. Around 9:00 p.m., I will have a light snack. I think I will have some herbal tea with a biscuit.

Quebec, October 17, 2006

I resume my writing project

I had a good night. I fell asleep without even having the time to turn off the light. I was so eager for the next day.

This morning, before I started writing, I reread what I had already written during my stays in New York.

So, my grandchildren, I continue this journey, back into my past. I hope you still continue to pay attention to me. I love you.

Part Eleven

My marriage to Jacques, in July 1979

For the wedding date, I chose Friday, July 13, 1979. It seemed to me the ideal date. It coincided with the construction holidays; Jacques would also be on vacation, and I would take time off at the same time. The wedding was scheduled to take place at the Saint-Jérôme courthouse at 3:30 p.m. The choice of Friday required us to organize two receptions: the first for family members in the afternoon of the wedding day, and the second the next day, Saturday, July 14, at 6 p.m. for all the guests.

Jacques and I went to buy our clothes, the rings, as well as the children's clothes. He wanted to control everything, as usual! For the occasion, I had suggested bringing his little brother Frantz from Haiti, which he accepted. Frantz arrived in Canada a week before the wedding.

Two weeks before, I had decided to bake the meat-filled puff pastry and the wedding cake myself. During my work breaks, I made a shopping list of the necessary ingredients.

Four days before the wedding, I began preparing the dough for the pastries and the cake so that everything would be ready for Friday the 13th, the wedding day. I was handling most of the preparations alone after work, with the children helping as they could. Given their very young age, it was out of the question for me to ask them for more help. I managed to make a large and beautiful wedding cake.

Members of both our families had come from New York and Philadelphia for the event. On the wedding day, surprising incidents occurred. The children had gone to play at the park with their cousins from New York. In the house, everyone was busy with something. As for me, absorbed in the preparations for the reception and the wedding, I couldn't check everything at once.

Jacques, on the other hand, was in a very bad mood. I didn't know why. Aunt Nadia had prepared a breakfast for all the men, albeit a little late, but they were well served and ate well. Despite everything, Jacques, as usual, was not satisfied and did not speak to anyone.

The ceremony was scheduled at the Saint-Jérôme courthouse at 2:30 p.m. When it was time to dress the children, one of them was nowhere to be found. It was Jacques' niece. We searched for her for nearly two hours. The police were even notified. She was eventually found in a field near the park, sleeping under a tree. I found it strange and thought to myself, "Friday the 13th!"

We were a bit late, and Jacques was very irritated. After getting dressed, he simply went to sit in the car that was waiting to take us to the ceremony.

But in the end, almost everyone was present at the Saint-Jérôme courthouse, including Sister Berthe, my adoptive mother, and my sister Irène.

Noticing that I was sad, Sister Berthe tried to comfort me: "Don't be sad, for God is watching over you. Ask Him for joy." During the ceremony, my mind was elsewhere. I tried to find an explanation for Jacques' bad mood. Yes, we were late, but it was due to circumstances beyond our control. I also questioned the relevance of this marriage. In short, I was extremely confused.

After the ceremony, we had our photos taken in Terrebonne. Back at the house, there was a small reception with champagne and pastries. The guests seemed to be enjoying themselves. As for Jacques and me, we left for our honeymoon at the Mirabel Hotel.

During the trip, Jacques hardly spoke to me. Upon arriving in the hotel room, he suddenly found his voice. He began accusing me of spending the entire day taking care of other people instead of taking care of him. He was so offended that he didn't make love to me that night.

The temperature in the room was too high, which kept me from sleeping. Out of frustration, I turned the air conditioning dial the wrong way.

The next morning, we returned home. There, he felt better because, deep down, he thought he had hurt me by not making love to me. It would have indeed affected me if I hadn't experienced the same thing before. In my first marriage, the same incident had happened. I truly don't know why it repeated itself on my honeymoons. It remains a perfect mystery, and I must assume I'm not superstitious enough to not see some sort of sign in it!

At home, my family and I began preparing for the second reception. There were many people. Everyone had a great time and danced a lot. Around 11 p.m., I went downstairs to find that all the guests were dancing, packed together like sardines with partners they didn't know, while I, the bride, wasn't dancing. I thought to myself, "My wedding is bringing them so much joy." I envied their happiness. Anyway, I like seeing people happy around me.

The next day, my family had to return to New York. It had been planned that we would spend two weeks in the United States with the children. We all left together for a pleasant trip. Jacques was in a better mood during the trip; as for me, I did my best to make sure he wasn't unpleasant. He was in good spirits because, according to him, he had control of the situation.

Twelfth Part

Life after the marriage

After the wedding, everything was fine. The children went back to school. Jacques' brother came to live with us. To help him make some money, I asked one of my neighbors, who did home sewing, how to rent a sewing machine. She promised to provide all the necessary assistance for me to do so.

I discussed this with Jacques and told him that I would teach his brother the basics of sewing and how to use the machine. He agreed with my idea.

So, Frantz started working. He was very smart. When I was away and needed information, he would go to my friend Farah, who gave him advice. Everything went well. However, Frantz had a very irritable temperament. For the children, I wasn't worried because I knew that when Jacques and I weren't home, Frantz would be there to greet them when they came back from school. On that point, I trusted him.

I worked a lot, and Jacques sought to claim all my attention. He wanted to show his brother that he was "the boss." He continued to make me suffer and imposed unacceptable treatment on me. And since I was always tired, I would cry over small things; I just didn't feel good about myself.

One day, Madame Bélisle came to see me. After observing me, she told me, "You're not doing well!" Then, she suggested that I stop working in my current state. She advised me to get a sick leave.

I managed to gather the relevant information on the subject. I spoke to my doctor and employers about my exhaustion, and I told Jacques that my doctor had prescribed a break from work for a while. To convince him to accept, I had to promise that I would work from home to make up for the amount that would be deducted from my salary.

Well, this leave of absence complicated my life even more, both personally and socially. Jacques pushed me to accept much more work for his brother, but he wasn't very quick with the sewing machine, and moreover, he lacked experience in making clothes.

I worked non-stop; it never seemed to end. Sometimes, I would spend the whole night sewing while everyone slept because the work had to be delivered the next day. I no longer went out. I had to take care of the house, the children, Jacques, and his brother.

The two of them always kept each other company when Frantz took a break from work. Passionate about mechanics, they spent their free time repairing their cars. Jacques would completely ignore me, even if I spoke to him. My sister, who came to spend the day with me once, was deeply shocked by the amount of work I had to do. She helped me as much as she could.

She also advised me to take a women's improvement course. She offered me this course as a birthday gift, commenting, "It will do you good to think a little about yourself."

I attended the course. I even participated in a fashion show in front of an audience of 500 people. At the end of the course, all participants received a certificate of participation. It was a very fruitful experience that I will remember for a long time.

As the days passed, Jacques' brother became more arrogant and petty. Our neighbor Francesca, whom he had tried to court, quickly put him in his place. After he also made advances toward me, I reported him to his brother, who eventually decided that it was time to throw him out.

In the meantime, my sick leave had ended, and I returned to my regular job. We returned the rented sewing machine and kept the one we had purchased. I continued doing a little sewing, as I had decided to work just two days a week with the sick for a while, until things got back on track. I accepted less exhausting orders; I made full dresses and also took orders for cakes and meat pies.

Max had learned to sew a little, despite being only 10 years old, and he occasionally helped me. He did a good job. In fact, everyone pitched in. That was Jacques' rule: you must earn your bread by the sweat of your brow. At 6 years old, Natasha already helped me with baking. Max worked much more than his sister. In addition to assisting me, he helped Jacques with his mechanical and construction work; he mowed the lawn in the summer and shoveled the parking lot in the winter. It was a lot for a little one. He did it so that his father would stay in a good mood. We all had to do the impossible to keep him satisfied, which created a heavy pressure in our house.

Thirteenth Part

Brief stay in Quebec of Jacques' mother

When Jacques' mother arrived in Quebec, she went to stay with her daughter, Claudette. She didn't visit us often because Claudette opposed it. A strong animosity had developed between her and Jacques. I didn't get involved, as it was none of my business.

Soon after, Jacques' mother returned to Haiti. In the meantime, Jacques and I had decided to make a family trip to Haiti. I hadn't been back in ten years, and I wanted the children to know their country of origin. Max was eleven years old, and Natasha was six. I also wanted a little respite as I was exhausted.

Fourteenth Part

Our stay in Haiti, July 1980

Since Jacques and I were entitled to a month of vacation for the year, we decided to spend three weeks in Haiti. After purchasing the tickets, I informed my sister Claire, who lived in Haiti, that I would be returning to the country with my husband and children.

We judged that it was preferable to take the plane from New York, from Kennedy Airport, with American Airlines. We took the precaution of renting a car to travel around Haiti. We drove to New York and spent the night at Aunt Dadia's house, who then drove us to the airport the next day. It was during this trip that I met my unknown friend again. (A character from my first book, *Tales of a Multifaceted Life*).

Upon our arrival at the Port-au-Prince airport, several members of my family were waiting for us. The children felt uncomfortable, as they weren't used to the constant hustle and bustle that characterizes the country's main airport.

We didn't stay long in Port-au-Prince. Once we picked up our luggage, we drove to Miragoâne. At that time, the country's roads were not as pitiful as they are today.

Once in Miragoâne, the children started feeling better. When they met their cousins Ketty, Jeanne, and little Claudine (a ward of my sister Claire), they appeared very happy. I took them to see my godmother Ruth, my mother's friend, who lived three houses away from my sister. It's amazing how this woman, despite her old age, was still very lucid and strong! She had a small store (equivalent to a convenience store) where my children got into the habit of going to drink Haitian cola every day. It made her happy; she spoiled them a lot.

Every day, my sister Claire would drop a basket of tropical fruits on the table. The children appreciated the gesture. Max preferred mangoes, while Natasha enjoyed Haitian cola and other fruits. She had some difficulty with food, but fruits and cola seemed to suit her better. My sister was worried that she might get sick.

We had a wonderful time in Haiti. We visited Aquin, the city of Les Cayes, Cavaillon, and Camp-Perrin. My brother-in-law George was a contribution collector in Aquin and owned a large two-story house. We stayed a bit longer in this city because of the beautiful beaches.

Sometimes, we left the children in Aquin and went to Les Cayes or Port-au-Prince. Jacques' parents lived in Les Cayes. At that time, they were still alive. In Les Cayes, we went to Gelé beach and various countryside parties.

Jacques and I went dancing once in Cavaillon with his nephews and my brothers. We had left the children at Jacques' mother's house in Les Cayes. We were eight people in a small Honda; the road was very bumpy, so we had to walk part of the way.

We arrived at the party at 3 a.m., and it was still crowded. In Haiti, dance parties end at 6 a.m.

We then went to church to pray, after which we took the return route, using a safer path this time.

During our stay in the country, Jacques was full of energy. He was surrounded by his family and friends, and making love with him was enjoyable. The children were delighted to see him in a good mood.

On our return to Aquin, the car was packed with people. The boys sat in the back, with their feet hanging outside. I thought they were taking serious risks, but they mocked me. Jacques told me, "Enice, you know where we are. In Haiti, a free country! We do whatever we want here."

Then came the time to return to New York and Montreal. I felt sad, and the children did too. But our duties and our adopted land were waiting for us! Just before our departure, Max got sick. Since he had a high fever, we gave him aspirin, but he continued to run a fever. His health greatly concerned my sister. In the plane, I kept an eye on him. As soon as we arrived in New York, we took him to the hospital. They ran some tests, but nothing was found. It turned out to be an intestinal infection. The doctor prescribed a liquid diet for him, and by the next day, he was feeling better. We then returned to Montreal.

When we got back, we still had a week of vacation left. We took the opportunity to rest and spend some time with the children. We felt nostalgic for the country. For me, the nostalgia lasted a week. Jacques, on the other hand, remained obsessed with the idea of returning, to the point where he started selling some of the furniture in the house. He wanted to go back to Haiti no matter what. He had lost the desire to work. He was melancholic, criticizing everything. Things started to go very badly.

Four months after our return from Haiti, we learned that his mother had passed away. He was devastated by the news. When he found out the circumstances of her death, he became even angrier. And it was on us that he took out his grief and resentment. We became his scapegoats. Life in the house became unbearable. But life went on. It had to. We had our respective responsibilities.

In life, you must know when to stop and when to turn the page.

Sixteenth Part

Failures in my writing process

October 18, 2006, Quebec

Last night, I had difficulty falling asleep. I turned over in bed several times without being able to close my eyes. I was nervous. My mind wasn't at peace; my head was too full of ideas competing for space. I wanted to write, but I felt incapable of putting a word on the page. The ideas were too tangled, too disordered in my brain. I then decided to read a little to relax. I read Chapter II of my favorite book: *Go Where Your Heart Leads You*. The pages I read calmed me, and I fell asleep around 1 a.m.

That morning, I struggled to get up; my legs were in great pain. I had to hurry to make it to breakfast on time, as the doors of the dining hall closed at 9:15 a.m.

After breakfast, I went to say my morning prayer at the chapel. Then I went back to my room, tidied up a little, and now I'm sitting at my desk, ready to continue narrating my tumultuous past for you, my dear children and grandchildren.

Fifteenth Part

The adoption of the children

In the meantime, life goes on. The holidays are over, and I return to work. The children started school again in September. Jacques, on the other hand, returned to work with little enthusiasm. The only thing that seems to satisfy him is sex. I give him that to comfort him. We talk about adopting the children to change their names. We discuss this with them, and they are very pleased with the idea. I make an appointment with my lawyer about this.

Jacques accompanies me to the meeting. The lawyer explains how he will proceed and shares his fees with us. We need to provide him with the marriage certificate, my divorce decree, and the birth certificates of the whole family. As usual, I brought everything. He asks for half of the amount to start the process, and the rest will be due on the day of the hearing. He will have many procedures to follow. First, a social worker will visit the children to check if they are being well-treated. The children's biological father will also be contacted. Although Tony is not Natasha's biological father, he will need to be contacted for her as well. When I had my daughter, I was not yet divorced from Tony, which is why she has the same last name as her brother, Tony's last name.

Leaving the lawyer's office, I was surprised to learn that Tony would have to be informed of our actions. It makes sense for Max, whose biological father is Tony, but I hadn't expected this for Natasha.

I wasn't worried about the social worker's visit because I knew my children desperately wanted to change their names. In fact, they had asked me several times. I wanted them to have my last name, but since I was married to Jacques, I carried his last name. I had, however, kept my maiden name as well.

One day, a social worker called to inform me that she intended to meet with the children alone, without my presence. She set up an appointment for the afternoon when they would return from school.

I spoke to Max and Natasha. I explained to them that a lady would come to meet with them to check if they felt good at home and if Jacques was treating them well. I told them that this meeting was about changing their names. They were very happy about it.

On the day of the meeting, the children seemed very excited, especially Max. Natasha didn't fully understand yet; she was calm, as usual. When the social worker arrived, I welcomed her in the living room, then left her with the children. I went downstairs to take care of my tasks. I wasn't concerned, trusting entirely in God. I simply thought, "Let His will be done!"

The social worker stayed with the children for 45 minutes. After she left, Max told me everything they had talked about.

What my son shared about his biological father surprised me greatly. How could he remember all those details? He revealed that he had always feared Tony. He recalled how Tony would hit him, how he wouldn't keep his promises, especially about a bicycle he had promised but Max never received. Max assured me that he was very happy with us.

Tony's lawyer had asked him to provide proof that he had always paid child support and exercised his visitation rights. Since he couldn't provide any evidence, his lawyer made it clear that his chances of winning were slim.

On the day of the hearing at the Youth Court, I felt very nervous. I didn't want to meet Tony. The judge and we waited for him for nearly 45 minutes, but he never showed up. Finally, the judge announced his decision: "Since the father did not appear in court, I declare that the names of the children Max and Natasha will now be changed to the name of Jacques and their mother Enice." And that's how the children succeeded in changing their names.

The entire family was happy with the result. Looking back, I still wonder if all of this was worth it, especially since now, I exclusively use my maiden name.

A Reflection

Are there certain actions we take at a certain point in our lives that do not protect us from unfortunate repercussions, leaving us to ponder the consequences?

A Small Pause

12:10 PM

I'm going for lunch and will resume my narration a little later. We are still in Saint Louis de Terrebonne. I am eager to finish.

I return at 12:50 PM. I walk for 15 minutes inside the monastery because it's raining outside. To clear my mind, I read two chapters of *La Dame aux camélias*. It is the first novel I read in my youth.
I'm now ready. Let's continue.

Sixteenth Part

Summer Activities

Despite everything going on in my married life, I didn't let anything show. Everyone around us believed we made a perfect couple. Friends would tell me they liked seeing such a successful marriage as ours. They'd mention how my husband was always in a good mood and very kind, how we frequently traveled to New York, etc. At those moments, I would quietly nod in agreement with their comments.

In fact, I was the one who organized most of these trips because I loved traveling, and these getaways allowed me to clear my mind and take a break. That's also why I agreed to fulfill all his whims and satisfy his fantasies—otherwise, nothing worked.

Summer was my favorite season. Since I worked every other weekend, I could plan family outings, like going to the beach, participating in picnics, etc. Sometimes, Jacques' sisters and their children would come from Philadelphia and New York for the summer holidays. We'd take them to tourist attractions. They seemed to enjoy the vacations immensely. As for me, I used these times to escape and recharge, to continue my life with Jacques.

During these summer vacations, we also went to New York and Philadelphia. The children loved these trips. My son even had a t-shirt with the American flag design. He would always wear it while traveling to stand out.

There are women who never show their despair, so much so that those observing them don't notice their state of distress. They seem joyful, travel as a couple, go on family outings, and it seems like they're swimming in pure happiness! I say this from experience because I was one of those women.

An Attempt at Objectification

However, one must not forget that a particular phenomenon explains this behavior: the family secret. We are caught in a vicious cycle with no way out; we gain weight, feel stomach pains, and experience various kinds of discomfort. We constantly try the impossible to keep our husbands happy at all costs. The sacrifices made include accepting their behavior, even continuously satisfying their sexual fantasies. Doctors fail to detect our illness, even though it's very real. The inner wound is intense; nothing is right, but we cover it all with a thick coat of indifference to ourselves.

And one day, we wake up. We tell ourselves that it's certainly not too late to take control of our lives and strive to survive, not gaining anything materially but regaining our dignity and personal integrity. Some, less fortunate than me, haven't made it. One of my good friends lost her life in the process. I acknowledge that experiencing painful and unhappy marital relationships is not exclusive to women. Men also fall victim to this, but I remain convinced that what I suffered as a woman could never be imposed on a man by his wife.

Seventeenth Part

The Low Point: Jacques Loses Confidence in Himself

Jacques was a hard worker back when we lived in Saint-Louis-de-Terrebonne. At the end of each year, his company would lay off employees for two or three weeks. He would use this time to do home renovations. Acting like a man possessed, he kept himself constantly busy and became extremely aggressive whenever I advised him to slow down and take a break. He always found something to occupy himself with at home or elsewhere.

He was still in charge of the budget. Thanks to my small personal savings and the ten dollars he gave me each week, I was able to sign up my daughter for a women's improvement course and figure skating lessons, and my son for baseball and athletics activities. Jacques, on the other hand, was completely indifferent to all this. He claimed that such activities were suited for white people, not for his children. I remember the Athletics Association had recruited Max for one of the professional teams because he excelled in long jump and running. Jacques refused to allow Max to join, saying it was a waste of time.

When I pointed out that the amount he gave me each week was not enough, he would respond thoughtlessly: "If it's not enough for you, there's nothing I can do about it." In other words, I should make do with the little money he gave me. He always ended the discussion with this phrase: "End of discussion." I knew he made good money and could give me more, but I didn't dare insist.

He ordered me to cancel our life insurance policies, the children's education insurance, and the health insurance policies on our personal loans and the mortgage for the house. He claimed it was money wasted, money that the banks used to make substantial profits. His words shocked me: with this attitude, he was jeopardizing the children's future.

At the same time, our credit cards were almost "maxed out." Personally, I didn't engage in costly or ostentatious spending. But I wasn't lacking in desire. However, I was extremely cautious in my purchases. Jacques, on the other hand, believed it was essential to go shopping every weekend and "fill up" our credit cards. He would invariably buy personal clothes and tools. After trying on his clothes and shoes and asking for my opinion, it would be the end of the afternoon. It was at that point he would express surprise that I hadn't bought anything for myself. He'd offer to let me choose something, but I didn't have the energy left. His reckless behavior had completely disoriented and exhausted me. I'd go home empty-handed.

Our credit cards, I remind you, were at their limit. One day, I told Jacques we should stop using them. I found a way to pay them off and eliminate the debt, provided he agreed to stick to this resolution, which he accepted. I asked my sister to help us with the repayment. She wanted to know why I had used these cards so recklessly. I had to keep the truth from her to get her cooperation. I made her believe that these expenses had been for the children and the house. That's how I managed to repay all our credit cards.

Still not cured of his depression, Jacques continued to spend excessively on home renovations. But I couldn't figure out where the money was coming from. I hoped, at least, that he hadn't started using our credit cards again.

He rebuilt the terrace at least five or six times. He made modifications to the basement and repeatedly worked on the parking area. I was left bewildered and helpless.

But life went on. And our expenses continued to spiral out of control. A decisive change of course was necessary.

I tried to convince Jacques to move to Montreal. "We can sell the house," I suggested, "and buy a new one in Montreal. Since the children go to school there, it will be less tiring for both them and us. Plus, we will reduce our expenses."

Although he was becoming increasingly nervous seeing our budget overruns, he refused to consider my suggestion. I didn't know what more to say.

My health, meanwhile, was not good: I was experiencing heavy bleeding with every menstruation. During a visit to my doctor, I learned that I had a fibroid. He sent me to a gynecologist for confirmation.

As for Jacques, I described his condition to my friend Nélia's husband. They had more experience in married life than we did. Nélia's husband suggested that Jacques come to visit him. A few days after their meeting, Jacques told me that our house would be put up for sale. "I'll demand a good price," he said, "because I've worked hard on the renovations."

I called a real estate agent, and we took the necessary steps. At the same time, we started looking at houses for sale in Montreal. It was March, and the move was planned for July. Our agent gave us a list of available houses based on the neighborhoods we had chosen. This almost daily house-hunting exploration proved to be, as expected, extremely exhausting and all-consuming. Several factors had to be taken into account, including the net amount from selling our house. It felt like we were participating in a poker game.

We received an offer from our third visitor. He thought the house was very clean and in excellent condition. The offer led to a counteroffer, and the real estate agent tried everything to get us to accept it. We were aiming for a higher amount. We eventually reached an agreement with the buyer. I must admit, however, that the amount we received was significantly lower than what we had wanted; it didn't even cover the expenses related to the renovations made on the house.

For what came next, we were floating in indecision: was it better to buy a new house or rent an apartment? With all the stuff we were carrying, an apartment wouldn't be suitable. Moreover, we didn't have a very large budget. We only had enough money for the down payment on a duplex and to do some renovations.

Our choices in Montreal were very limited. We eventually found a modest duplex on Hénault Street. It was a 4½ with a basement. Max could have his own room in the basement. It was very large and included a room, a bathroom, and a playroom. The house had a large kitchen, a large dining room, a large living room, two large bedrooms, a small bedroom that needed renovation, and small bathrooms.

Hénault Street is close to Boulevard Gouin and the Rivière des Prairies in Montreal-North. The neighborhood also has a park. It was really a nice area, which I loved.

October 18, 2007

The End of My Stay in Saint-Louis-de-Terrebonne

Tonight, I feel a bit exhausted, but at the same time, happy because I am finishing the narration of my ten years of life in Saint-Louis-de-Terrebonne. It is in this city that I lived the longest with my family. I don't completely regret it, but I wouldn't want to relive the same experiences for anything in the world; they were too painful. I must thank God for helping me get through it all, safe and sound.

It was at the end of this overwhelming event that I definitively left behind this part of my life in Saint-Louis-de-Terrebonne.

An Interlude

October 19, 2006 — 10:00 AM

My dear grandchildren, before I continue my story, I would like to tell you a bit about the present.

This morning, I had difficulty concentrating. After returning from breakfast, I opened the window to air out the room a bit. I, too, needed to breathe a little better. The weather outside is not good. A thick fog, which prevents me from seeing the other side of the shore, covers the river.

Nature, as a whole, still seems wonderful, with trees half-covered in golden leaves. Autumn, in its own way, is a very beautiful season, but it's not my favorite. Yet, when I reread the notes I wrote during my stay in New York, I realize that it is in the fall that inspiration comes to me easily; I truly don't know why. Perhaps this season helps me escape or surrender, just like the trees let their leaves fall.

I will continue my writing, my dear ones. I know you're eager to read about the adventure of that house on Hénault Street in Montreal, but I can't concentrate enough to write. The process is laborious, and all my thoughts want to spill out at once; my head is full, and I'm suffering from it. I'm going to meditate a little and walk around the monastery corridors for a few minutes. See you later.

Chapter 6

Our Move to Hénault Street

Part One

During the ten years spent in Saint-Louis-de-Terrebonne, we had accumulated many belongings, which were difficult to pack and transport. For example, we had to account for two dining rooms, two living rooms, four bedrooms, the small outdoor shed, Jacques' tools, renovation materials, tiles (since Jacques had removed them from the parking area at the Saint-Louis-de-Terrebonne house), etc. In short, it was quite a sizable inventory.

Jacques refused my suggestion to hire a moving company. In his opinion, the trailer and the two vehicles we had would be more than enough.

As with our previous moves, my two children, a friend of Max, two sons of Jacques' cousin, my friend Anièce, as well as Viviane and her eldest daughter, came to lend a hand. The drive to the new house took 30 minutes. Jacques had planned and organized everything very well, so the move went quite quickly.

Since I had already cleaned the new house, all we had left to do was set up our furniture and belongings. As for our house in Terrebonne, since we had always kept it very clean, the new owners moved in on the same day. The new owner's wife even thanked me for leaving her a home in impeccable condition.

Thanks to the help of our friends, we managed to settle in all-in-one day. It was a long, exhausting, and draining day! At dinner, Jacques' cousin surprised us by serving delicious Haitian food: fried pork, rice with red beans, macaroni salad, and green salad.

Once our friends left, a new family life began for us. We had new neighbors. We had a small shed in our backyard. However, we didn't have parking spaces. Jacques decided he would build one. An area for a car behind the house allowed us to unload the car in the meantime. The house required significant renovations, especially on the outside.

It was an old single duplex with two apartments. An external staircase had been built for the tenant upstairs. Our apartment was on the first floor. It had a balcony at the front and a veranda at the back, which we later transformed into a second dining room. The bedrooms were very small, especially the ones upstairs. However, the kitchen and living room were quite spacious, and the finished basement included a large bedroom, a bathroom, and a playroom.

A Pressing Pause

12:00 PM I stop writing to try and clear my thoughts. In this Hénault Street house, we spent 11 months, and so many events took place that I'm struggling to put them in order.

I'm trying to gather them, but they're pushing each other to be told first. I feel like I have a computer in my head that's being attacked by viruses and can't defend itself. I feel overwhelmed, and the tunnel I'm in is narrowing more and more. I will go have lunch and take a break; I'll continue later.

1:00 PM: I'm back from lunch. Due to a conference being held, there were many people in the cafeteria today, which broke the usual monotony of the place, usually so quiet. As for me, I had calf liver, a dish I enjoy.

Part Two

Beginning the Work at Hénault Street

It's summer, and we need to start the outdoor renovations as soon as possible because this season doesn't last very long. In the meantime, one of my friends, Isabelle from New York, called to announce that she would be visiting me for a short stay with her daughter, Milène. It's been a long time since I've seen her. I let her know that she and her daughter would be very welcome at my home.

Everything is going well for our family. Jacques is very busy with the renovations, and I occasionally give him a few ideas. As for our sexual relationship, he is never too tired to engage in it when evening comes.

For me, on the other hand, these physical relations had become extremely painful, and sometimes I would cry. He would tell me, "Like this, you can't stay at peace to receive my penis; stay there, my dear, and hold yourself well!" I would reply that I was in pain in my private parts. He would respond, "I'm not in pain; hold yourself well and take it properly! I don't want to hear any more complaints from you." My God, how I suffered! I went to see a doctor and shared my lower abdominal pain, as well as a previous hemorrhage crisis. The doctor referred me to a gynecologist at the Notre-Dame Hospital.

I scheduled an appointment for the following month because I had anticipated that Jacques would need my assistance with the house maintenance. A plan had been made. We had decided to cover the veranda with treated wood and then paint the bricks at the front and sides of the house in a red color, cutting their edges with a complementary color—gray, like cement. It was a very meticulous job.

One Friday in July, my friend Isabelle and her daughter arrived from New York. We were happy to have them. Isabelle was meeting my husband and children for the first time. They introduced themselves and exchanged a few words.

I explained to her that we had just moved in and that we were planning renovations. Jacques and the children were supposed to go buy wood the next Saturday. Isabelle and her daughter decided to join us for the purchase of materials, and we took the opportunity to show them around the city. We took them to the Oratory of Saint Joseph, then to a store to buy nails. We had a good time.

My sister was expecting us for dinner. We went to her house without Jacques because I didn't want to disturb him; I brought him his dinner instead. The next evening, Sunday, my friend and her daughter left, happy from their trip.

The renovation work began that Sunday morning: Jacques started by demolishing the wooden wall of the veranda. We soon realized we needed insulation material. Jacques went to buy it. It was urgent: the wall couldn't stay exposed for too long. My husband had to go back to work on Monday at 3 PM, so he requisitioned everyone to help him. That day, he worked extremely fast, like a robot. By the end of the day, he had almost finished: removing the rotten wood, cleaning up, installing insulation, and starting to prepare the boards for the next day, just before heading to work. My son helped him a lot.

The next morning, I went to work. When I returned, I was astonished: the house had completely changed its appearance. Jacques had managed to lay the floors and did an excellent job. When he called me from work, I congratulated him.

After telling me that only the painting was left to do, he added that Max had been a great help. Max, in turn, proudly described how he had assisted Jacques. I thanked him with a hug. The next day, Jacques and Max did the painting and applied the finishing touches to the veranda. Everything was becoming even more pleasant to look at as the work progressed joyfully.

In the meantime, Max and I had asked Jacques to draw something on one of the walls of his basement room, which my husband agreed to, provided, he said, that Max worked well at school and helped his father with the house renovations!

The so-called "construction holidays" had arrived. My little nephew Marco, the son of my brother Alain, came from New York to spend a month in Montreal. His stay was to be split between my sister's house and mine. Most of the time, Max took him out to entertain him; Natasha didn't like going out and preferred to keep me company at home.

Jacques had started painting the brick walls at the front and sides of the house. The joints around the bricks also needed to be painted. This delicate work required painting skills.

There was so much to do that I decided to take a month off to assist. With the children on vacation, they, their cousin Marco, and I painted the joints with small brushes. Jacques built a parking space at the front of the house and was able to lay the pavers. After two weeks, all the exterior renovations were completed. Now, all that was left was to redo the bathroom.

Part Three

Agents Lurking

The bricks looked so new that the appraiser thought we had replaced the old ones. When he arrived, he asked, "Did you just change the bricks?" I answered affirmatively. He said it was a good job. As soon as the renovations were finished, real estate agents rushed to suggest that we sell our house. But we were not at all interested in selling.

A few months before the move, Jacques had bought a Nissan van, which allowed us to transport our belongings as well as the materials. I had sold my little mini, and Jacques had given me his Toyota car. This was the first time he had bought a brand-new car. Previously, he always repeated that buying such a car was a waste of money. This time, I had managed to convince him otherwise.

I asked him to wait a bit before starting the bathroom renovation, but he refused. I tried to explain that we needed to take a break and some time off: that the children needed free time to go have fun with their cousin and friends! He replied, "They can take a little rest, and I will continue alone." Still, we had managed to organize small outings with them, such as going to the beach on Sundays.

Meanwhile, my little nephew complained that his heel hurt, especially when it rained. We spoke to his parents and advised them to take him to a doctor once he returned to New York.

One day, while Jacques was renovating the bathroom, a real estate agent rang the doorbell. He wanted to tour the house for a possible sale. Jacques warned him, "I'll give you a tour, but I'm not selling! I'm happy here. Also, I haven't finished the renovations." When the agent left, he confided in me, "When I've finished the renovations, if a seller agrees to sell the house for the price I want, I will sell it and buy another one." He hoped to recover the money we lost in the transaction of the Terrebonne house. I advised him to be careful. He promised me that this time he would be cautious.

He had almost finished the bathroom, only needing to replace the oil heating system with electric heating. In the meantime, the children were delighted to stay in Montreal. Each was settled comfortably in their room, with Natasha always with her cat and Max drawing on his wall. They were happy. As for me, the hemorrhage crises returned. I couldn't wait to see the gynecologist.

A New Pause

3:10 PM:

And that's it! I'm taking a break.

6:30 PM:

After dinner, I take a walk to the chapel to thank God for allowing me to regain my inspiration and to feel less pain in my back and legs.

Part Four

Summer and Fall (1987 and 1988) on Hénault Street

It was August, and I had three weeks of vacation. My cousin Viviane, whom my sister and I consider our own sister because our mother was her godmother, came to visit. In 1972, she had a little girl named Marlène in Montreal. Since she lived alone, she had sent her daughter to her sister Fabienne in Haiti for her education. She received a good education.

At the age of 12, she decided to bring her daughter to Montreal to live with her. During those 12 years, she had another child, a little girl named Marie, whom she loved dearly. Marie was a bit spoiled by her mother, which was normal since she was the only child in the house. When Marlène arrived in Montreal, her sister Marie was six years younger than her. It was difficult for Marlène to adjust to her sister, as well as to her mother whom she barely knew. The mentality of people here was different from that of people in Haiti.

She had many problems. In fact, her daughter Marlène was much taller than her. This little girl was very spoiled by her aunt Fabienne in Haiti. She did whatever she wanted and could have anything she asked for. It was tough for her; she was completely lost. We couldn't expect her to understand everything at once. Her mother told us that once, she had to climb on a chair just to talk to her eye to eye.

In the second week of August, Viviane, Marlène's mother, came to the house to ask me: "Would it be possible for you to keep Marlène at your place during your vacation to see if she could change her behavior and understand life in Montreal?" She told me that since my daughter Natatsha and Marlène were about the same age, Natatsha could go out with her and explain how life works in Canada. Before Viviane made her request, I had already thought of that because, usually, Marlène came to stay with us on weekends. Honestly, between her and my daughter, it went very well. I accepted her request. The next day, Marlène arrived at our house, very happy.

Natasha was thrilled; the two girls slept in the same room. Natatsha considered her like her own sister. I was delighted that she was with us. I took her to the stores, explained to her what to do and what not to do, the respect of people, etc. I spoke to her like a friend, with no aggression. But I didn't let her do whatever she wanted. My daughter also helped her.

Marlène was a cheerful little girl. Every night, she would tell horror stories to the children before bed. At that time, she would immediately fall into a deep sleep while the others, including my daughter, stayed awake and had nightmares.

I remember one day, I sent her to buy a loaf of bread at the corner store. She came back saying, "I don't understand the people here. After I paid, I was short two cents, and the lady didn't give me the bread. She told me to go get the two missing cents. I told her some nonsense. Because in Haiti, when the amount is not complete, people say, 'You'll bring the money next time.'" I explained to Marlène that we weren't in Haiti here; there are laws, and they must be respected. Everywhere you go, at school, on the street, etc., and even at home, there are laws. Otherwise, there would be anarchy. My daughter and I worked a lot with Marlène on her education. To the point where my daughter was jealous of her. Natatsha was unhappy.

One day, when she couldn't keep her secret anymore, she said to me, "Mommy, you love Milène much more than me." I took her in my arms while whispering, "You know that you are my darling little girl. Right now, Marlène needs me and you too. It's just for the time being while she gets herself together." She smiled and went away satisfied. After my vacation, I took her back to her mother; Viviane was happy to see her. She lived in Rivière-des-Prairies, and during her stay with us, not once did I let her go to her house.

Two weeks later, Viviane came to bring me a beautiful gift, crystal cups; she wanted to thank me for what I had done for her daughter. She said that it was like having a different child return to her. She mentioned, "I don't know what to say, there are no words to thank you." She gave me a big hug and then thanked Natatsha. I was delighted to see her joy. I was also proud of my daughter and myself. She had really made room for Marlène.

For me, what I did in helping my cousin was just like many other things I've done, and I would like to do even more. I believe that every human on earth should have their share of happiness, especially children.

Present

October 20, 2006

This morning, I passed by the chapel to ask God to calm my pains. Last night, I had a lot of pain in my legs. It felt like something was moving inside my left leg. Yet, I walk and do exercises. Today, it's better. I also asked God if He could help me with the terrible nightmares I struggle with at night. I prayed for Him to send an angel to rock me to sleep and inspire more beautiful dreams. And I thanked Him.

Tonight, I am determined to continue my writing activity; I will go to bed when I feel very tired. I must take advantage of it while the inspiration is still here.

Part Five

My Fibroid Surgery

Family and domestic life continued without much change. Max had finished his drawing on the wall; it was beautiful, depicting a breakdancing group. Max met his friends much more often than when he lived in Terrebonne. In August, I went to see my gynecologist at Notre-Dame Hospital. After running tests, he told me that I needed surgery because I had a fibroid the size of a grapefruit. He also asked me if I wanted another child. I answered no, but he advised me to discuss it with my husband before making a final decision. If I wanted another child, I would have to have it before the surgery; I would need to stay in bed for the duration of the pregnancy. It was a "think about it" situation! The gynecologist asked me to let him know our decision as soon as we made it.

Throughout the whole drive back home, I couldn't stop thinking about the contents of my conversation with the doctor: fibroid... surgery... child. It was all confusing my mind.

When I got home, I informed Jacques about the specialist's instructions. "For me, the surgery is a yes," he responded. "But for the child, it's a no." I then expressed the following comment: "The children have grown up and are in their studies; they won't be able to help me at home. On your side, you are always busy, and I would also need to stay in bed for the duration of the pregnancy. So, I would be the only one doing all the domestic tasks. I won't take on that responsibility." So for me, too, the answer was no. In fact, I was forced to decide for him, because he kept repeating that he didn't want any children who would cry from morning to night.

Anyway, the next day, I called the doctor to let him know that I was ready. He promised to let me know the date of the surgery soon. At the end of September, I went into the hospital. I had taken a sick leave. On the day of the surgery, I asked the doctor to do his best to avoid removing my ovaries.

The surgery went well, but when I woke up, I felt such intense pain that I screamed like a madwoman. The specialist had to administer a high dose of painkillers. The next day, I was so drugged that I had hallucinations: I saw snakes everywhere in my room, coming down from a fern pot that my sister Irène had brought me. Hearing my terrible screams, a nurse called the doctor, who recommended lowering the dose. The next day, I was feeling better. The doctor came to see me and informed me that he had removed one of my ovaries because it contained a cyst. My anemic condition forced me to stay in the hospital for two weeks. It was a bit long, but it allowed me to rest. Upon leaving the hospital, the doctor prescribed three months of rest.

When I returned home, Jacques and the children were very attentive toward me. Max and Natatsha prepared dinner as best as they could. Jacques made me porridge with plantains, which he believed would help restore my strength because of its vitamin properties. My sister also came to visit me frequently. Some friends also came to visit. As for me, my extreme and total dependence made me very stressed. I couldn't even take a bath on my own.

Three weeks after the surgery, Jacques already wanted to make love. I refused. But I had to struggle against his repeated advances, to the point that my stitches came undone a little, and I had to go back to the doctor about it.

But Jacques kept coming back. I asked him if he wanted me dead. He answered no, but added that sex was his "vitamin," which I found disgusting. I can't describe what happened then. I became aggressive: these forced sexual relations repulsed me. I cried for no reason. I believe I went through quite a long depressive state. Two painful months went by before I felt good in my own skin again.

I resumed my domestic activities, but I didn't return to work, as the doctor had prescribed two more months of leave, which suited me perfectly. I was receiving an amount from the health insurance, but the family budget remained very tight.

Max, who was now in the 5th year of high school, had to study more to get good grades. His sister and I strongly encouraged him. He had still managed to get a girlfriend, and I had recommended to Jacques, but in vain, to give him some advice on romantic relationships. Eventually, I had to talk to him about it myself.

One day, I entered his room and explained, in my own way, "the facts of life," what concerns relations between the sexes. He thanked me with a hug. Since then, I've been very comfortable talking about these topics with my two children, and I've never regretted it. It's the same now with my grandchildren. They, who are still very young, can also benefit from the sex education offered at their school.

In November, we celebrated Max's birthday, which created a joyful atmosphere throughout the family. I was feeling better and better and was in an increasingly cheerful and joyful mood.

As for Natatsha, she still stayed very calm, most of the time in the company of her cat. One evening, it didn't come back. The next morning, when I opened the door, I saw it almost completely disfigured. Not having heard it scream, my daughter approached. Upon seeing the state of her cat, she rushed into her room and refused to open the door for the whole day. She didn't go to school. I called the SPCA to come and take it.

It was horrible to see. Here's what happened: the cat, wanting to warm itself, had taken refuge under a car, and the fans had crushed its face. My daughter's heart was broken. She refused to have another pet as a companion. She remained marked by this event.

Jacques was still working a lot on the house; he was able to redo the electrical installation in August. He had also rebuilt his semi-truck, which he wanted to be stronger and more spacious. It had exhausted him; he was also in a bad mood because he didn't appreciate my performance in bed. Our new house was quite small, so he couldn't hurt me as much, for fear that my daughter would hear us, as her room was adjacent to ours. I then realized that he was hurrying to finish the renovations in order to sell the house. The same real estate agent, by chance, had resurfaced. He wanted to examine the house again, which, he assured us, he could sell for a very interesting price.

After his visit was finished, he renewed his offer and promise. Jacques then told him the amount he wanted to obtain. From then on, our house was put up for sale, provided the visits began after the renovation of the bathroom was completed. Two months later, the property was indeed sold, at the price Jacques had determined. The result of the transaction put him in a good mood. We now had to look for a new house. Our task was now easier since we were already in Montreal.

In the meantime, I received a visit from my childhood friend Doris, who lived in Haiti. She stayed alternately at my place and at my sister's. She offered us to buy a piece of land that she owned in Haiti. The offer interested Jacques, who was already thinking about purchasing land there. The land was located in Chalon, in the suburbs of Miragoâne, my hometown. Doris gave us a good price. After our move, we promised her that we would return to Haiti during our summer holidays to finalize the purchase. Thanks to the money from the sale of our house, we bought the land, significantly reduced our credit card debts, and made a substantial payment toward the purchase of our new house.

Because we quickly found a very spacious house located very close to Hénault Street, more precisely on Lamoureux Street between Boulevard Gouin and Léger. It was wonderful. We were fulfilled.

It was a three-bedroom bungalow, completed by a four-and-a-half in the basement, which was already rented. The entire property, in very good condition, included, among other things, a parking area and a shed. But our monthly expenses were going to be much higher than our previous house, even considering the basement rent. According to Jacques, we would succeed in balancing our budget, to which I agreed. We now had to pack our things for this new move. This time, I found the task quite burdensome, especially since I wasn't quite fully recovered from my surgery. However, I didn't want to show it. I really felt exhausted and disgusted, especially by sex. I did it without interest. Just to please him. He didn't suspect anything, as long as his needs were satisfied.

I mainly wanted to avoid him being in a bad mood with us. It was better this way. Sometimes, I wondered if I would manage to hold on. To this question, I got no answer, or at least I refused to find one.

Another Break

It is 10:00 PM. I am preparing to go to bed. Before that, I went to get a cup of herbal tea, "Night of Dreams," to help me fall asleep. I will drink it just before going to bed. Good night, have sweet dreams.

October 21, 2006

This morning, I went to breakfast late. The service ends at 8:00 AM. I arrived at 8:10 AM. I was all alone in the cafeteria. "Madam, take your time," the service manager whispered to me. I had a light breakfast: a slice of brown bread, some pieces of cretons, and fresh grapes. Then, three prunes, a coffee, and grapefruit juice. I feel good today, I don't know why. I don't feel any pain. I must say I had a good night. I dreamt, but no nightmares. I went to the chapel this morning to thank God for the good night and asked Him to grant me another good day. The weather is nice today; after lunch, I will go for a walk.

10:00 AM Before continuing my writing, I am rereading some passages I wrote yesterday.

Sixth Part

Max's Misadventures

The children continued to grow, and at the end of every summer vacation, we would always go to New York to buy them new clothes and shoes. They loved these trips. They were also very proud to show off their beautiful and exclusive clothes when they returned to school.

Max had bought a nice white leather coat with black and white checkered sleeves. It was a very comfortable coat. Once, while going to school with his friend Nelson, a very strong boy, Max was attacked by two boys who tried to steal his coat and shoes. He ran for his life to escape them. When he returned home, he told us what had happened. Jacques decided to show him how to defend himself. Having already practiced karate, he knew what to do. He gave the two boys an electric cable that they had to tie around their waist; if they were attacked, they would untie the cable and use it to strike their attackers. Jacques had them practice and repeat the necessary movements.

A few days later, Max and Nelson were indeed attacked by a gang of thugs, and they managed to easily defeat them by beating them with their cables. Since then, no one has dared to harass them.

In my opinion, parents must always stay attentive to their children to protect them and prevent them from being negatively influenced by strangers.

Max Gets His Diploma

Before our move, Max took and passed his final secondary school exams. He was happy with his results, and I was proud of him. Natatsha, for her part, was overjoyed. "Mom," he told me, "it's thanks to you and Natatsha that I succeeded, you both helped me a lot to get through." He then kissed me to thank me.

He asked both me and my daughter to accompany him to his graduation dance, which two of his friends, Jacob and Joséphine, siblings, would also attend. I drove everyone in my car.

Along with their classmates and friends, they had a great time during the evening. Natatsha was the youngest in the group, but she looked tall for her age. She stayed at the table with me throughout the evening.

I had promised Max that I would organize a small party for him at our new house and invite the family's friends. Jacques had approved my plan. I kept my promise: the party took place, and all the participants were extremely satisfied.

All in all, I recognize that we had a happy year in this house, despite the occasional small inconveniences. At least, I enjoyed a year that was a little calmer than usual. Now, it was time to move to a new house once again.

Chapter 7

Our Move to Rue Lamoureux

Part One

This time, the move was easier, but in this new house, we already had a tenant. Although the previous owner had offered him some money to cancel his lease, he decided to stay. Let's say, rather, that he left while pretending to still occupy the premises. He didn’t give us the keys, and he didn’t answer the phone. To get to the bottom of it, Jacques went, on the day of the move, to take a look through the patio door: no one was in the house. After breaking the lock, he entered. Bags filled with trash were scattered all over the floor. Jacques took them out, and we took possession of the place.

As the children had grown, they were able to actively participate in the move this time, along with Max's friends and, as before, my brother Robert.

My cousin Viviane, her two daughters, Marlène and Milly, and my friend Anièce also gave me a hand. This time, I was going slowly because I had been a victim of a workplace accident in June. I had to be very careful with my spine.

We didn’t put everything in place on the same day. The men first arranged the furniture. For the rest, I suggested to the girls to just clean. Marlène, for her part, stayed at the house for three days, during which she and my daughter provided very valuable help.

I loved this house as soon as I arrived, I felt good in it. It was a semi-detached brick house, with a very high-ceilinged basement, a large front balcony, and a wide raised staircase at the entrance. There were flowers on both sides of the front of the house. A paved parking area stretched from the sidewalk to the shed at the back of the yard. The back part of the yard was partially paved. The rest of the yard was covered with grass with a maple tree in the center. It was exactly what I wanted, the property was to my taste. In fact, I had spotted it just by chance. While taking a walk alone, I had seen the sign. On a scrap of paper, I immediately wrote down the seller's name and phone number.

The property included three bedrooms, a large kitchen, a large dining room combined with the living room, which had a fireplace. The bathrooms were not very large. But the hallway and kitchen floors were ceramic. We had plenty of storage space. The very large basement contained a washer and a built-in dryer. To complete it all, there was a living room and a storage area for Jacques' tools. In short, it was the house of our dreams. We didn't want anything more. The children and I were fulfilled. I believe Jacques was too, but he didn't say anything.

And there you have it, I've given you as accurate a description as possible of this house in which I've kept dramatic and unforgettable memories.

A Pause

1:00 PM. I'm back from lunch. I had planned to go for a short walk, but I realize the weather has changed. Instead of going out, I climb the stairs to the third floor. It feels good. I want to make progress on my writing project, and since inspiration is here, I better take advantage of it.

This morning, I had to call my son at his work to get some information about a specific event, because I didn't want to make any mistakes. Max answered my questions very satisfactorily and helped clear up my concerns.

At lunch in the cafeteria, there were many people. I ate until I was full with the following choices: sole fillet, carrots, vegetable soup, broccoli. For dessert, a fruit salad accompanied by an herbal tea.

I don't feel stuffed, and that's just fine. If I'm describing what I eat, it's because every time I communicate with my daughter and son-in-law in the evening, Patrick always asks me, "So, what did you eat today?" He always wants to know what I did and what I ate during the day. I find this concern touching on his part.

Let's now get back to my story.

Part Two

Our Trip to Haiti to Buy Land

Everything was fine in our new house. Since it was very spacious, the children could invite their friends over. My sister now came to visit me a little more often, along with Viviane and her two daughters, including Marlène.

Every week, Marlène came to help me with my cake and pâté orders. In return, I gave her a little money. We get along very well. My children's friends loved coming over. I often talked to them and gave them good advice.

Jacques and I had to go to Haiti to buy the land. I had made the reservation for August. But before that, Jacques' sister Raymonde, who lived in Philadelphia, came to spend a few days with us.

We had to prepare for the trip to Haiti. So, I took a vacation one week before my departure, during the last week of July. We left for two weeks, leaving the children at my sister's. They came back to the house from time to time.

Unlike our first trip, we left Canada in complete peace of mind. My friend Doris, who was selling us the land, was waiting for us at Port-au-Prince airport. I had, in any case, taken the precaution of writing to my sister Claire to inform her of our arrival.

Doris took us to Dikini to her large four-story house, a real palace. Driving along the National Route, you can see the house on the mountainside. It was impressive to see it from so far away. I couldn't help but exclaim, "This is not a house, it's a hotel!" She objected, "It's really my house, not a hotel." She seemed amused by my astonishment.

At the village of Carrefour, she took a small bumpy street full of large stones and holes. When we arrived in front of her house, she pressed a doorbell, and a guard came to open the gate. A large German shepherd immediately came to meet us. It was happy to see its owner again, but it looked at us menacingly. Doris signaled it to lie down and asked the guard to take it and tie it up. She wanted to know if we were afraid of dogs. I answered affirmatively, while Jacques said the dogs didn't scare him at all. She still advised him to be cautious because she had four trained dogs to defend the residence and put intruders to flight; they were released every evening.

The yard was made of cement. In front of the house, there was a flowerbed and small coconut trees, about five feet tall, loaded with coconuts. It was the first time I saw this species. The cars were parked in front of the house, with the gate always closed. The entire property was enclosed by a nine-foot-high wall. The pool was visible, despite the presence of several cisterns.

The interior of the house was extremely luxurious. All the floors were furnished. Our friend took us to the room she had prepared for us. It had its own bathroom and all the desired amenities.

We then went down to one of the dining rooms that led out to the balcony. I almost fainted as I ventured out onto it. I'm afraid of heights, and it takes me several minutes to adjust. From there, I could see the entire capital. It was wonderful to contemplate everything. The sea, the port of Port-au-Prince, enormous houses and tiny houses, huts, tents, etc. A particularly disconcerting sight: humble cottages next to this imposing residence. You could see, a little lower down, children who were ragged, almost naked, waiting for the wealthy to throw their garbage behind the fence so they could hurry to check what they could recover. That was how they ensured their survival.

The country has come to this. And Haitians seem to be getting used to it:

"We can throw anything down, they kept telling me, someone will go and pick it up right away!" I felt great sorrow for these poor people, but I couldn't change their fate.

The trip had been long, and we were hungry. Our host invited us to eat, promising to show us the house a little later. She also introduced us to her two children, Richard and Yvette.

She had the maid prepare a delicious dinner: fish, white rice with red bean sauce, bananas, potatoes, yams, and a salad made of beets, tomatoes, and lettuce.

We had a wonderful meal, even though Doris thought we hadn't eaten enough. Then we talked about everything and nothing. Doris's husband hadn't returned from work yet; as a captain in the Haitian army, he was assigned to the National Palace as bodyguard to President Jean-Claude Duvalier.

Third part

Doris's House

In the backyard, there is a fruit garden. You can find all kinds of plants: avocado trees, coconut trees, mango trees, sapodilla trees, banana trees, etc. No outsider can enter without permission, and the dog house was installed right next to it.

Let's start with the first floor. Since the house is built on a mountain, this floor is smaller than the others. It's actually the basement; it includes the conventional kitchen, the laundry and ironing room, the servant's quarters, and toilets with a shower.

On the second floor, there is a storage room for bulk food, a large room with a living room, a very luxurious kitchen with a stove, refrigerator, etc.; a large dining room, all with a view of the balcony, these rooms being open. Next to this, there is another dining room, this one enclosed, and a large living room with matching furniture. On the balcony, there is another living room. During my stay there, I showed Doris how to better arrange her furniture and paintings to enhance the entire space even more.

On the third floor, there is the master bedroom, very spacious, richly furnished, and equipped with a bathroom, as are all the other bedrooms in the house. There is also, on each of the three main floors, an entry hall with large glass windows and an exit onto the balcony with a view of the landscape, as well as plants in almost every room. After the entrance hall, there is the children's room; then other rooms for guests and toilets. The whole thing is really very beautiful.

After the tour of the house, we headed to our room to unpack our luggage.

Our host had warned us that she would come to get us once her husband returned. After unpacking, we changed while enjoying a panoramic view of the city. Just observing the people below, I had had enough. It was like being in a movie. A few minutes later, I went to sit in the small living room on the balcony.

When her husband arrived, Doris called us. We met him while he was having dinner with his children and his wife. For us, she had prepared a good grenadine juice. She insisted that I eat some good bread. I promised her I would eat it tomorrow. Since she kept insisting, I took a small piece of bread with butter, and Jacques did as well.

After making sure we had had a good trip, the captain told us that we were welcome at his home while also repeating his wife's warning about the dogs. He clarified that it was he who personally fed them, ensuring they didn't get used to anyone else. He served them raw meat to make them fiercer.

The conversation continued on the balcony. Doris warned us that we would leave very early the next day for Miragoâne to go see the land.

That evening, Jacques and I made love: "You can't tell me you don't want it," he whispered; "We're in Haiti, the weather is beautiful in our country." I replied: "You don't need to be in Haiti to do that." He then added: "We're alone on this floor, you can scream as loud as you want, no one will come to your rescue. Anyway, I warn you, you're going to need all your energy because I feel in top form."

I slept well. It was the sound of roosters and donkeys braying that woke me up. We had breakfast before hitting the road. My friend had advised us to wear sportswear, a hat or cap, and to wear proper shoes. The trip would last just one day, during which we would meet with the notary and go greet my sister Claire, her husband Georges, and their child. We also planned to stop by my brother Raymond and his wife, who lived in Nouvelle Cité.

We got into her convertible jeep, and she handed the wheel to Jacques. The jeep, I don't know why, was without a roof, despite the blazing sun and the dust from the road. We still had a great time. The music was turned up full blast, which delighted Jacques; he is always in a good mood when visiting Haiti, and many pedestrians stopped on the road to watch us pass by.

The drive lasted an hour and a half. The roads were in pretty good condition. As soon as we arrived, we went to examine the land, located in Chalon, almost at the entrance to the town of Miragoâne. The manager guided us through the site: a large plot of four acres, with fruit trees and coconut trees, millet plants, pigeon peas, tomatoes, yams, banana trees, etc.

The examination of the property, which extended to the edges of the national road, was quite long. And we liked it. I still tried to lower the price, but in vain. She said no. We eventually gave in. Doris then informed the caretaker that we were the new owners of the land. She had included a small thatched-roof house for the caretaker and his family.

According to the established terms, the caretaker would give part of his harvest to the owner. As my friend had announced her arrival, he had prepared some sacks of corn, millet, etc. We drank coconut water and ate the coconut flesh. It was truly paradisiacal.

We then went to the notary, who recommended that we return in a week to sign the purchase contract. We stayed the rest of the day in Miragoâne: I took the opportunity to visit my sister and my brother. Then we returned to Port-au-Prince.

Upon my return to the capital, I immediately called Christèle, a good family friend, whom my sister had asked me to run some errands for. She promised to come visit us the next day and take us to visit a farm owned by the Sisters of Wisdom in La Plaine. Christèle taught deaf-mutes and lived with the nuns in Port-au-Prince.

We went to the farm. It was a real one; in addition to other fruit trees, we saw all kinds of animals in their enclosures or chicken coops: pigs, goats, oxen, chickens, etc. The farm was very organic, with an efficient irrigation system. We were served a very simple meal.

I returned, amazed, to my friend Doris's house. It was fantastic to discover such a modern farm in Haiti.

A brief pause

5:20 PM It's time for dinner.

6:30 PM After finishing dinner, I stopped by the chapel after calling my sister. She informed me that there was melting snow in Montreal. But here, in Quebec, it's not snowing. It's raining. It's humid, I can feel it in my bones. I won't be walking around my room tonight because I want to make progress on a writing project.

The rest of my stay in Port-au-Prince

My cousin took us to visit some neighborhoods in Port-au-Prince. In the meantime, her husband, whose car, a Toyota, was having mechanical issues, had told us that no mechanic in the country could repair it. With the help of the servant, Jacques managed to get it working after two days of work.

We participated in several interesting activities during our stay there. I certainly didn't get bored. But one event, in particular, is worth mentioning. We were supposed to, as planned, return to Miragoâne to finalize the purchase of the land. Richard, one of Doris's brothers, had invited us to Cholette, a small locality on the mountainside, a few kilometers from Miragoâne, accessible by a very bumpy, narrow, steep road bordered by cliffs on both sides. The trip, which lasted at least three hours, could only be done in a jeep.

We left the capital very early. Upon arriving in Miragoâne, after quickly greeting my sister, we went to the notary to sign the land purchase contract and pay for the transaction. Doris's brother was waiting for us. Without wasting time, we headed for the road to Cholette. Richard was driving: we had to cross a large river. Richard, driving very fast, had turned up the music from the Martinique group Cassave (kasav). The mood was joyful, but I was very scared; my heart was racing, and I closed my eyes to avoid looking at the cliffs.

The cliffs were very deep on both sides of the road, and since I'm afraid of heights, I could barely breathe and remained silent. Jacques, of course, suspected my intense feeling of fear. When we arrived at our destination, I let out a sigh of relief and thanked God for being alive.

Richard showed us pigsties and coffee plantations. What fascinated me the most was the majesty of the green mountains, with trees suffocated by their leaves: the sound of the wind rustling through them created music that no one can enjoy unless they are truly in tune with nature.

I was in ecstasy. I felt like I was in paradise. The rustling of the leaves, the cries of the birds. The sound of the streams joined in to create this music that enchanted me. And the beautiful blue sky with its white clouds, so close to us, giving the impression of being in space.

Around me, people were talking, laughing, and feasting. And I was euphoric, I felt like I was in heaven. I don't know if I'll ever relive this experience, but I certainly don't regret it.

Yet, when I was little, I spent my summer vacations here in Cholette. Back then, I would always go play in the woods. I probably loved those beautiful moments, but I couldn't describe what I felt at that age.

We stayed overnight on the mountain. The next day on the way back, Jacques drove the jeep. Noticing that he was driving recklessly, I scolded him: "You know, Jacques, my children are waiting for me in Montreal, I wouldn't want to die in a stupid accident." He understood my message and immediately stopped his reckless driving.

Three days after our return to Port-au-Prince, we went back to Montreal, our heads filled with moving and everlasting memories. During our stay there, we had always lived the lifestyle of the rich and famous: home massages, gourmet food, hair salons, pedicures at home, etc. My hosts' children were very calm. The little girl had a very skinny cat. "Why don't you feed it?" I often asked Doris. She would invariably reply: "He has to hunt to eat; if I feed him, he won't hunt. Let him go hunt outside." What a shaky response! This stay in Haiti at Doris's will remain forever etched in my memory.

Fourth Part

The Return from Haiti: Chronicle of Rue Lamoureux

Jacques had been living in a state of nostalgia since our return from Haiti. He was clearly unhappy, but he did everything he could to keep things going well within the family. The children had resumed their studies. Max, enrolled at Dawson College, was doing his schoolwork in his room. Natatsha, who was in second secondary at Roberval, had started making friends.

Upon my return to work, I suffered another accident; it was actually a relapse. I had to stop working again to undergo physiotherapy treatments: the specialist diagnosed me with a herniated disc. After the treatments and an assessment by the CNNST, I was informed that I simply needed to change careers. The entire process, from the initial steps to the decision from CNNST, took at least a year. I took a secretarial course for a while. At the end of the training (in May 1989), just one week before I was to return to work, I was involved in a car accident. Once again, everything had to stop.

Before this accident, things were going fairly well: since I wasn't working, I had more time to take care of my family, and Jacques was very happy about it. I still had to be careful with my back due to its extreme sensitivity. On this subject, the doctor had recommended that I reduce the frequency of my sexual relations, which didn't sit well with my husband. According to him, he was the only one who could determine when and how to make love to his wife.

The CNNST had granted me substantial financial compensation. Given my physical condition, I decided to get rid of my small non-automatic car without power steering. I bought a lovely 1971 light blue Mercedes, which was much more comfortable for my back. When I later suggested to Jacques that we invest in a six-unit building, he flatly refused, claiming that this type of business generated too many complications, especially due to the "delinquent" behavior of certain tenants.

On Saint-Gertrude Street in Montreal-North, not far from the credit union where I had deposited the CNNST compensation, there was a travel agency. The idea struck me to surprise Jacques by buying us plane tickets to Miami,

Florida. I chose a date that coincided with his vacation week and made a deposit, with the remaining balance to be paid in three days.

Jacques was away when I returned home, so I called my sister to share the good news. "For once you're thinking of yourself," she exclaimed, "I think you're doing well." Then she added, "Do you remember I promised to give you a gift if you managed to lose weight through the strict diet you had decided to follow? Well, I'll pay for your ticket!" I was delighted.

When Jacques came home, I revealed my surprise to him. He went wild and furious. "What am I going to do in Miami?" he shouted at me. "Why do you want to go there? Who put this stupid idea in your head? You're wasting your money, go get the deposit back. I'm not going to Miami." I replied that it was too late since the tickets were already paid for. I then added that my sister would pay for my ticket. "That's even worse!" he exploded. "So it's her who put this ridiculous idea in your head. No. There's no way I'm going to Miami!" As I repeat his words, I can still hear his arrogant and disdainful tone. I burst into tears. I couldn't understand his attitude. I just wanted to make this man, with whom I shared my life, happy, and this was the response I got.

I was overwhelmed. He even took me to my sister's to ask her to cancel the trip. "Enough is enough," I said to myself, "this time I won't let him control me!" I then declared that I, Enice Toussaint, was ready to go alone; I had even called my friend Doris in Florida to tell her I was coming.

Doris, you may recall, is the woman who had sold me a plot of land in Miragoâne, Haiti. She had bought a house in

Florida and, for security reasons, had moved there with her children.

My husband looked at me, surprised by what I had just said. My sister then intervened and said that if she had decided to do without a husband, it was because she hadn't seen any good examples of one around her. It was then that Jacques suddenly asked about the date of my departure. He then announced that he would accompany me, since the trip would last barely a week. I remember that upon our return to Montreal, he gave me this explanation: "The only reason I went to Miami was because of what your sister said about not wanting a husband." I remained silent: it was clear that his arrogance had taken quite a blow.

During our absence, the children, now older, alternated between staying at our house and at my sister Irène's. On the day of departure, he was more eager than I was to board the plane. It was a very pleasant trip. Jacques spent a lot of time in Doris's pool and kept saying, "I don't regret coming." As for me, I was extremely happy to reunite with a dear childhood friend, Josie, whom I mentioned in my first book. When we were at the same boarding school, we shared our most intimate secrets. We hadn't seen each other for 28 years. She was thrilled to introduce me to her children and her husband; in fact, I already knew him from when I was a very young girl.

Josie had organized a big dinner to celebrate our reunion, which moved me deeply. I had a deep affection for this upright, gentle, and sincere woman. She is no longer with us, and I still think of her.

Anyway, this stay in Miami was a success; it did me a lot of good, and it's partly thanks to the fact that I promised myself I would use my own money for the trip.

Fifth Part

Events and Renovations of the Lamoureux House

For nearly a year, things went quite well. This can be explained: I was very cautious in my actions. Jacques, on his side, in addition to his regular job, was taking on small renovation contracts. But, due to a work accident, he had to stop for at least three months. Like me, he was receiving 90% of his salary. We had more or less converted the large room next to the dining room into an office, and I had placed my computer there; this way, I could continue practicing typing and computing.

During his sick leave, Jacques made changes to the basement to create a room for Max. By eliminating a bedroom upstairs, he planned to enlarge our bedroom and the bathroom. I thought the idea was good. But without warning, he moved Max to the basement and began demolishing. I wanted to understand the reason for this urgency. "You know, I don't have much time, we need to do this quickly," he explained. I then accompanied him to buy materials: the whirlpool bathtub, the medicine cabinet, plumbing items, etc. We temporarily placed them in the living room and dining room. Jacques made the changes to the bedroom and bathroom, and he drilled a small door between the bedroom and the bathroom, but without putting up drywall on the separating walls.

He then proceeded with the plumbing installation for the bathtub and the electrical supply. Putting off the floor repairs in the bathroom and the bedroom, he installed the bathtub, sink, and a built-in shower. "For now," he said, "you can use the bathroom. I'll finish the rest later." He tried to reassure me by insisting that the essential work had been done and that the rest would be finished soon.

One day, while checking my bank account, I noticed that a lot of money was missing, and many withdrawals had been made. When I tried to ask Jacques about it, he simply said he had used the money to buy what he needed.

I had noticed that he had recently acquired a very sophisticated graphic camera, a video camera, new tools, etc. I reminded him that he had rejected my suggestion to invest in real estate, had initially refused my Miami trip plan, and that I hadn't bought anything personal with the money I had deposited in the bank. He didn't respond. I suddenly remembered that I had lost the money I had paid for purchasing bedroom furniture, because he didn't like it. I then decided to buy the same furniture, this time without talking to him beforehand.

When I returned from the store, I calmly said, "You know, Jacques, I finally bought the bedroom furniture I really wanted." He stared at me and asked, "Where are you going to put it?" I replied, "In my room when it's finished. In the meantime, I'll leave it all packed in the living room, there's enough space." This wasn't entirely true.

My words made him so angry that he accused me of squandering money. "At least," I pointed out, "I'll keep a memory of the money I received as compensation for my back problem." He fell silent. But do you know what? The bedroom furniture stayed in the living room for almost a year.

Once the bathtub and shower were installed, Jacques no longer hurried to finish the bedroom or the bathroom; they became real dust traps. A few days before Christmas, while we were all at the table, everyone mentioned what gift they hoped to receive. "As for me," I said, "if you're planning to get me a gift, Jacques and Max, at least finish my bedroom. For me, that would be the best gift." Jacques took me at my word, and with Max's help, he managed to finish the room just two days before Christmas. As for the bathroom, it wasn't completed until two months before the sale of the house. So, we didn't have time to enjoy it, unlike the new owners.

Sixth Part

Turbulent Relations

Since my car accident in May 1989, Jacques' character had become increasingly unpleasant; despite my constant efforts to improve our relationship, he grew more aggressive. For several days, he barely spoke to me.

Jacques had evicted a tenant who was causing serious trouble and refusing to pay his rent. He then decided not to rent to anyone else, which led to an imbalance in our budget. Max had moved into the basement apartment, and we had converted a second living room. Jacques turned one of the bedrooms into a tool storage room and set up an office in the game room. This way, everyone had their own space.

It was after all these changes that Max, probably inspired by his painting in his room, created three beautiful paintings that he exhibited at his college. After the exhibition, he gave one to me, another to my sister Irène, and kept the last one for himself. As for Natatsha, she began going out more often. She participated in the Miss Montréal competition and was ranked among the top ten. From that moment on, the atmosphere in the house changed. Jacques became jealous of the children. He constantly grumbled that I was spoiling them, that I was always kissing them, and that they were my favorites.

A New Breakthrough

A Return to the Motives of My Writing Project

Saturday, October 21, 2006

4:30 AM. I hardly slept last night. Around one o'clock, I started reading the journal I've been keeping since May 16, 1989. I had noticed that for the past few days, I couldn't move forward with my writing project, and I hoped that reading my journal would help me regain my inspiration. I read everything I had written from 1989 to 2000, noting that nothing had been written for certain years. As I relived these past events, I felt a deep sense of disgust. I was in pain, but I didn't cry. I prayed to God to cast out the demon that was causing me so much suffering, and I thought about the words my sister Irène's friend, Jean Martin, the psychologist, had said to me.

I remember that when I returned from New York during this period of writing, I felt ill without fully understanding what was wrong. I experienced strong feelings of nausea and was deeply saddened because I had just written a very painful part of my life and was unable to continue. In short, I was blocked and revolted. My sister had invited this friend for dinner and offered me to join them. I had not planned at all that I would confide in Jean. At the end of dinner, Irène left us alone in the kitchen. We sat around the island, a corner where our guests liked to gather to grab a bite or chat. Jean asked me to talk about my stay in New York. I revealed what had happened there: the circumstances of my departure, my hasty return, my anxiety attacks, and so on.

Speaking to me as a friend, he then shared these words of encouragement that have stayed etched in my memory, although I haven't had the courage to put them into practice since November 2004. I was so consumed with fear! It haunted me for two years, but I eventually overcame it through persistence, prayers in a quiet place, and writing.

But last night, as I reread these painful passages in my journal, I felt that fear take hold of me again, preventing me from moving forward with my project.

Here are, however, the precious words my friend, the psychologist, said to me. Who knows? They might touch other hearts as deeply:

"You should not say you feel guilty (because that's a judgment). No judgment! And don't think about what others will say; that will disturb your writing! Appreciate what you are now. And tell yourself you can claim this experience and write your story. Do the cleaning, get rid of the residues and waste. You start over, you move forward. Tell yourself: 'I have the power! The power over myself, over my writing, and over my emotions. It's not pain that is my mistress. I must control my pain, my experience.' Writing is an act of self-power. For example, when describing what happens to me, I relive the scene, but I'm not living it anymore. Through writing, I free myself and own it. You write the product of your experience. — You ate crap; it gave you this product. You've made 99% of it interesting. When you write 99% of things that hurt, it creates a recall effect. — You are the master of the situation. Don't let it swallow you, or you won't be able to tell the story. — When you write, you do a narration. — The narration (absence of judgment), repeating it, is a feeling of recall. — Repeating: 'I control my pain, I write it, I have power over it.' — You must decant! Decant the emotions. Go from pure state to emotion. — Reactions! You recover; that's relief. It's a purification process. You detect positive and negative emotions. There are no residues left; you've done the cleaning; you've done the vacuuming. You must say: 'I am in control. "

My sister, sitting in the living room, had been listening to our conversation without my knowing and had taken notes.

The advice from our psychologist friend comforted me immensely and helps me now to continue with my writing project, albeit without a plan.

However, I will need to modify the upcoming pages in the form of my narration: it will adopt the style of a diary.

7:15 AM

It is 7:15 AM. I am tidying my room and then going downstairs for breakfast.

10:30 AM. I am back. This morning, I attended Mass; on Saturdays, it is held at 8 AM. This allowed me to go before breakfast. Here, at the convent, the employees leave for the weekend. The nuns take over. They are not very young, so the service is slower. And we have lighter meals. I feel better now after the dizziness I experienced last night. I'm holding up. I'm ready to continue my journey into the past with you, my little ones.

The beginnings of my diary

Here are the circumstances that sparked my passion for writing and led me to start my diary.

One morning, I went down to see my son Max in his room. I was feeling an immense sorrow and needed comfort. When I arrived, he was finishing up some work for his course. Noticing that he was absorbed in his thoughts, I was about to turn back when he invited me in, saying he would resume his research later. I began describing to him how I was suffering from the treatment Jacques was subjecting me to at home. While listening, he nodded in agreement with my words. And as I cried, he tried to console me by wishing that Jacques would change his attitude and that everything would eventually return to normal.

"But I feel like I don't have the energy to keep enduring all this," I whispered. He made me sit next to him and urged me to tell him a part of my childhood, the trials I had gone through after my mother's death, and the suffering I endured with Tony, his biological father. Then he intervened: "Mom, with everything that's happened, you should write a book about your life. You never know, your testimony could help people." I told him that I had always wanted to write, but due to a painful incident, I had not been able to fulfill this aspiration.

Unknowingly, my son had just awakened a desire that had been dormant in my inner consciousness. I thanked him and promised that I would start my diary that very day. The fact that he had made me happy gave him great joy. We hugged, and I left him with a content heart. I knew I had taken some of his time, but it didn't bother him since he understood I was going through very tough times. That same day, I did indeed buy a blue notebook from a shopping center. I will never forget that moment. I kept the notebook carefully. Several times, I thought I had lost it, but I always found it again with joy.

Here is what I wrote in my diary on May 16, 1989. I transcribe exactly what I expressed. I must warn you that part of this content is already recorded in the preface of my first book, *A Woman Among Many*.

Dear Diary,

May 16, 1989

I've always had the idea of writing my life. I've often thought about it, but I received no encouragement. Now that my children are grown and I've begun telling them about my life, they support me a lot in this writing project, especially my son Max.

When I was a young girl, Sister Berthe, my adoptive mother, gave me a small diary for my thirteenth birthday. It was from that moment that I began to write a little about everything in my life. My second husband, Jacques, after reading my diary, decided to burn it because he found it too sad.

His action hurt me deeply. It was as if a part of me had died. But in the end, instead of bringing me down, his act encouraged me to refocus on my writing projects. It's going to be hard, but I still want to do it, especially since my car accident on October 5, 1989, when I almost died. Now, I would like people to wish me good luck and allow me to enjoy some moments of peace. (End of diary entry)

That is all I was able to write in my diary. That day, I couldn't write anymore. Events followed one another over the days until I had too much: the vase literally overflowed. I resumed writing my diary three months later.

In the meantime, I continued to do everything humanly possible to please Jacques and maintain a harmonious atmosphere in our small family. He had installed a motion detection system on the front and back doors to monitor the comings and goings of everyone. I constantly reminded the children to avoid disturbing him at all costs. He no longer worked for Canadian Steele. He was doing renovations on his own, and I took care of his accounting. He had even hired a few employees.

On my side, I managed the construction work and banking operations, wrote contracts, etc. Max had gotten a job at a restaurant downtown. This allowed him to buy small personal gifts and save some of his money to pay for his tuition fees. Jacques tried to hire him several times, but Max preferred to keep his job at the restaurant; however, since he worked in the evenings, he was happy to lend a hand to Jacques three times a week on his days off. In the meantime, he missed him; they often came to join him at the house.

When he went out, he would be back at our house by 11 PM: he followed the rules and avoided making Jacques angry. I remember that when he went out to celebrate with friends, when he came back home, he told me: “Mammy, I didn’t even have time to eat because I was afraid I’d miss the bus: I know my dad wouldn’t be happy.” For his 18th birthday, I organized a big party for him; I rewarded him for his good behavior, and he was thrilled.

Since I had completed the training prescribed by CNNST, I had to start working in my new profession as a secretary-accountant. My monthly salary was now lower, and the family budget was equally reduced. Jacques, on the other hand, continued doing renovation contracts. Work was plentiful. I, on the other hand, would have preferred to work outside, but he categorically refused. “With all the work there is,” he objected, “it’s better that you work for me.”

So life continued, but with a lot of constant tensions. One day, Jacques decided to give me control of the household budget, explaining that he no longer had time to manage it. I had prepared accounting sheets to make it easier to monitor the work. Every week, he would check the accounts; if a penny was missing, I had to provide a reason. This led to a constant climate of disputes and suspicion. And yet, when he had been in charge of the budget, I had trusted him completely; I never questioned anything, now I didn’t even have pocket money. Sometimes it was Max who helped me when the budget was deficient.

“Where was the love in all of this?” you might ask. Well, it was absent, but sex wasn’t! We had reached a point where we barely kissed. A brief gallop in bed, and that was it. Imagine a jockey mounting his mare and pushing her to the maximum of her performance capabilities.

I had reached the point where I no longer spoke and no longer thought about anything. I kept everything inside, and I had started quietly gaining weight again. In July, Aunt Dadia came to spend a few days here in Montreal because she was separated from her husband. We thought it would do her good.

Jacques' aggressive behavior had worsened. He thought Natasha was going out too often and that she loved sports too much, almost constantly engaging in basketball and other activities with her friends. I immediately understood that he was nitpicking. On my side, I no longer went out: he insisted that I always be at home in case he needed me, and I suffered a lot from this state of merciless slavery; I was doing things I detested.

During the "construction holidays," his sister Martine from New York, accompanied by her daughter Margo, came to spend a few days with us. We went out often with them. Since Martine had changed religions, she once asked me: "Enice, why do you wear makeup?" I explained that I've always loved wearing makeup, a practice I started at a young age. She then turned to Jacques: "I don't know why you let Enice wear makeup, she hasn't even finished her sentence." I replied, "Listen, dear, no one in the world can stop me from wearing makeup, not even your brother." Although she argued, she didn't bring up the topic again, and neither did Jacques. The subject was therefore definitively closed. For once, I had made my position very clear.

After Martine and her daughter left, I felt exhausted and depressed. I then thought, "My God, it's been a long time since I've written: I'm going to try to pick up where I left off."

Journal

August 7, 1989

Since May 17, I have stopped writing; I now spend long moments staring at the blank page. It is the silence around me. I do not speak to anyone. I feel alone and sad. I start thinking that there must be other things to occupy myself with in life.

I cannot communicate with my husband anymore; I no longer understand him (I am aware that I am repeating myself). This man has become extremely malevolent, and I suffer a lot because of it. I did have a brief calm period: during Martine and her daughter's stay, the latter, rather talkative, made us laugh a lot. Jacques seemed radiant in their company, while he was harsh, curt, and disdainful with my daughter and me. This situation was negatively affecting my inspiration: it was with difficulty that I managed to write a few words in my journal. After that, I wrote nothing for nearly six months. I simply observed the events and endured them.

Sixth part

Life continues on Lamoureux Street

When I was taking my secretary-accountant courses, it felt good to regularly meet new people. But lately, I don't go out anymore. I only take care of the house and especially Jacques' affairs. Anyway, he didn't like me going out. He would look at me with a disdainful expression, probably meant to make me feel guilty.

To make a change, I attended a meeting of the Miragoânais Association. We held elections for the board members. I was elected treasurer. The meetings were held once a month on Sundays, which gave me an opportunity to go out. He always accompanied me. I participated in several events: summer picnics, balls for Saint-Jean, etc. He didn't complain about it because he was always by my side.

We became part of a group that was setting up a travel agency for Haiti. This very important project gave us valuable business experience. If it hadn't been for some shady dealings, it could have been a great success, and the Haitian community would now be very proud of it.

Jacques and I were members of the board, him as assistant treasurer, and me as a counselor. The board had 12 people, and the company had about a hundred shareholders, each owning one to five shares. The board operated very rigorously and met every two weeks.

But a small group of five met separately every week. The president of the board knew very well how a travel agency worked. Everything was ready: the work plan charter, etc.; they just needed to finalize a few details. But there was one problem, one persistent question: the president's pay. He demanded exorbitant fees and excessive benefits. Fortunately, the money had been placed in trust, and to access it, two or three signatures were needed: the president's, mine, and another woman's; this third person always stood firm in her decisions. The president asked me, "Since Marie won't sign, I said, I won't sign either!" After that, he flatly refused to reimburse the shareholders.

Marie and I contacted the shareholders to reassure them, announcing that we would hire a lawyer to resolve the matter and the reimbursements.

The other board members were all very trustworthy citizens. Marie and I used our own funds to hire a lawyer. He forced the reluctant president to hand over the company's documents. Then, the board hired an accountant to handle the distribution. Everything was settled in one day. My friend and I signed and sent the reimbursement checks, including accumulated interest, to the various shareholders. Then we paid the accountant.

We came out clean from this venture. Most of the shareholders and board members were our friends. The president, it should be noted, had not bought a single share. That gave a good indication of his true intentions!

I have no regrets about this experience because it allowed me to meet serious people and make new friendships.

Seventh Part

My Second Car Accident; My Nephew Maki's Illness

For the children, everything was fine. Max had turned 18. I told him he could stay out a bit later. "We'll see," he replied. He still hadn't gotten a girlfriend. As for Natatsha, she was participating in many events and competitions.

In her first year of high school at Roberval School, she had won a bicycle by entering a drawing contest on the theme of cigarette use. She had taken a course in women's development, theater, and modeling. At the end of each school year, she participated in theatrical productions, fashion shows as a model, and various title ceremonies.

She also took part in several fashion shows in Montreal. It was at one of these shows that she met her friend Patrick. He was also a model. My daughter told me about the meeting, but without going into much detail.

At that time, I thought things were going well because I was encouraging my children in their various endeavors. But one evening, I went alone to a meeting. While crossing a street, another car violently hit mine on the passenger side, folding my Mercedes in half. I found myself trapped between the right door, unable to move. I felt excruciating pain in my back. The police arrived on the scene and called an ambulance, which took me to Santa Caprini Hospital. Jacques, who had been notified immediately, showed up there. After taking an X-ray, the emergency doctor decided to keep me in the hospital. The next day, I was in pain all over—my leg, back, etc.

After a series of tests, the doctor revealed that the damage was mostly internal. After prescribing anti-inflammatory medication, he placed a neck brace on me, a bandage on my foot and arm, and recommended hot baths. Then he sent me back home. I spent just one night in the hospital.

Back home, I was overwhelmed by a sense of revolt. I was in so much pain, but there was nothing I could do about it. It was autumn. The weather was bad. I no longer had my car, and the insurance company refused to repair it for a second time.

Everything was going wrong. Bad news kept coming. I learned that my little nephew from New York had just had a leg amputated. It was a huge shock to me. After his vacation in 1987, his father had him examined by a doctor because he was experiencing severe pain in his foot. The pain persisted. More tests followed, which revealed cancer. An emergency surgery was performed. I listened with deep sadness as Aunt Dadia, who had visited him at the hospital, provided all the details of the tragedy. She told me that it was the child, through his attitude, who gave the family courage. He didn't want his parents to cry; he was only 15 years old at the time.

After receiving this heartbreaking news, I closed myself off and started eating to comfort and console myself. I no longer wanted to talk to anyone. I stayed locked in my room, watching TV. I prepared dinner because I had to eat. I told Jacques to take care of the bills. I made his lunch, but there was always something missing. He wasn't in a good mood. He wanted sex, and I gave it to him to satisfy him, but I no longer cleaned the house like I used to. And every time I entered the bathroom, I felt disgusted. So, I decided to clear my mind.

One day, Jacques spoke to me very harshly and pointed out that the bills had mistakes and I had to redo them. "Redo them yourself!" I muttered. My sister, who he had complained to about my negligence, tried to reassure him, "Don't worry, it'll get better. She's just taking a break."

And one fine morning, while looking at myself in the mirror at my vanity, I was sharply surprised by what I saw. I had gained weight, my face without makeup was swollen, and I found myself alone at home. "Enice, my dear friend, what's going on?" I murmured. "You can't let yourself go like this. Make an effort." So, I took a bath, did my hair, cleaned up a bit, and made my bed so I wouldn't crawl back into it. Then, I went downstairs to check if everything was in order.

A little later, I prepared a nice dinner. When Jacques and the kids came home, I wasn't in my room. Busy with my computer, I was preparing Jacques' invoices.

Max was happy to see that I was feeling better; he was all smiles, as was my daughter. As for Jacques, he said to me, "Finally, you're deciding to come out of your shell?" I didn't react because I knew deep down he was happy too.

I slowly recovered from my little depression. I managed to repair my car, but I had to add a substantial amount to the sum the insurance company had given me.

A year passed without me writing a word in my journal. A few days later, I ventured to write the few lines that follow.

Diary Entry

November 4, 1990

This morning, I feel great. I want to do a lot of things. But, I still feel a bit depressed.

A lot of things have happened in my family recently. I wanted to get back to writing for a long time, but I didn't feel strong enough to do so. Yet, everything was in my head.

Since my two car accidents, I feel blocked. Yet, I'd like to get my life back to how it was before. Go out, work outside, meet other people. I think about it often.

Jacques didn't want that. He preferred that I stay at home. I don't know why. Whether it's out of love, jealousy, control, or cruelty. Sometimes, I felt like he didn't love us. I don't know what to think anymore. It's so complicated.

Sometimes, I feel like I don't know him, like he's a stranger. (End of excerpt)

Eighth Part

The Conflicts Between Natatsha and Her Father

A Family Secret

7:30 PM

Lately, my daughter often talked to me about her friend Patrick. They met during rehearsals for events. He had started coming over to our house. He would kiss me on both cheeks, very respectfully. He would occasionally bring me small gifts, very simple things, just to show that he appreciated me. These little gestures didn't bother me. Without any ulterior motives, I would show the gifts to Jacques. I never thought he would be so jealous. He was angry and kept repeating that he didn't like Patrick kissing me and giving me gifts. According to him, I should refuse them. I told him that he didn't need to worry, that Patrick was a cultured, friendly, and respectful boy. My soothing words did not calm him at all.

Yet, Max's friends, who were the same age as Patrick, also greeted me with kisses. I don't know why, but Patrick's gesture seemed completely unacceptable to him.

He was probably trying to find an excuse. For example, he claimed that Natatsha should avoid working. As for me, I had told my daughter that she could look for a job at the end of the school year. I wanted her to succeed in her last year of high school.

November 10, 1990

She told me important news. Here is how I wrote it down and commented on it in my journal.

November 10, 1990

Today, Natatsha revealed to me that she and Patrick were in love, and he had asked for permission to take Natatsha to the movies. I referred him to Jacques, after first mentioning it to my daughter's father.

He didn't take it well. He said to me: "I saw it coming—the kisses, the gifts—it was all to get accepted. I won't fall into these traps. My answer would be no." I warned him that anyway, Patrick would soon ask him directly and advised him to show some understanding and openness.

He was working in the basement when Patrick went to speak with him. My daughter and I stayed upstairs. Their conversation lasted a long time. I still don't know exactly what they talked about. Anyway, he gave his permission.

That first evening, the two of them came home late (they claimed they had talked for a long time in front of the entrance door). We were so scared that we thought they had had an accident. We called Patrick's mother's house, but they weren't there. Just as we were about to contact the police, they arrived, as if nothing had happened, and sat in the living room. Despite their explanation, we found their behavior completely inexcusable. My daughter was therefore punished by her father.

November 11, 1990

The next day, I told Jacques that his daughter and Patrick were in love with each other. He had a huge meltdown. I explained that it was normal for her age. But I understood him a little. Most fathers would like their daughter to remain their little girl forever.

However, he must realize that she is 16 years old. I think we're lucky that she confided in us. Anyway, it had to happen someday! Max is 22, and I don't even know if he has ever fallen in love.

I go back in time.

Since I told Jacques the news, life at home has become unbearable. I was the one taking all the blows. Patrick continued coming to the house without a care. Natatsha started going to his house too, which of course displeased her father. He complained to the whole family and our close ones that I was giving our daughter too much freedom, that I was excessively tolerant, in short, that I was a bad mother.

My daughter was outraged. She showed her rebellion by constantly doing the opposite of what her father told her. For example, he expected her home at 10 PM, she would come home at midnight. I tried to reason with her, but in vain. Jacques went after me and the boyfriend of his daughter, who was truly the target of injustices and accusations. I later learned from him that she was acting this way deliberately, to directly oppose her father's authoritarianism.

Sometimes, to calm the fury of Jacques, I would invite him to make love, even though I didn't want to at all. I knew he would fall asleep immediately afterward. Then I would quietly get up, go to the door, and deactivate the alarm to prevent him from discovering the time his daughter returned, all to avoid his insanity and insults.

One day, when Max and I were in the basement, and Natatsha in her room, I heard the noise of an argument. When I arrived in the room, Jacques was violently shaking his daughter and banging her head against the wall. "Jacques, no! No!" I screamed. "Don't do that! You're going to kill the child!" His eyes burning with rage, he quickly left the room. Rushing to the dining room, I called Max for help. "Max! Max! Come quickly!" Like a scene from a movie, the madman was breaking everything in his path. He threw the chairs and table from the kitchen onto the floor while rushing toward me. He pressed me so hard that the fingerprints from his fingers were left on my forearms. Max arrived and shouted at him, "Let go of my mother! If you want to hit someone, hit me instead!"

He immediately let go and returned to his room. My face was flooded with tears, while my son tried to comfort me. "It's the first time I've seen him like this," I kept repeating while sobbing. We went back to see Natatsha, who was also crying in her room! Like me, her arms were covered in bruises. Fearing Jacques' possible reactions, I begged the children to behave very well; as for me, I kept to myself to avoid problems. This painful experience made me realize that I didn't know the man I had married. I no longer trusted him. The children were extremely unhappy with the situation. Max, for his part, hardly spoke anymore: he tried to observe everything that was happening in the house.

However, Jacques was far from disarming. He frequently called my sister to defame us and present himself as the victim. Of course, my sister strongly contested his statements.

When I realized that his actions could drive me insane, I decided to personally reveal to my sister the mistreatment the children and I were enduring at home. During one conversation, she said to him, "You know, I know the whole truth about what you're making them endure. I don't want you to call me anymore." And after shouting, "They are martyrs!" she hung up. Jacques was furious. "So, you went and told your sister what's been happening at home?" he reproached me. I answered affirmatively and added, "I've always kept my promise not to tell anyone what happens at home, but I noticed that you started first. So, I'm doing the same thing as you. No hard feelings!"

The family was saddened by my husband's behavior toward us. Our life was no longer the same. It was autumn, and soon winter would come, dead seasons for renovation, Jacques was hardly working. Our credit cards had reached their limits after multiple purchases of materials Jacques made with them. He was only paying the minimum required each month. Our expenses exceeded our income. I then resorted to my last resort: my sister once again agreed to co-sign for a debt consolidation negotiated with the bank. Everything was paid off: credit cards and other loans. We only had one monthly payment to make in addition to the mortgage. But the amount of the mortgage was very high because of the excessive interest rates at that time. Moreover, we no longer had tenants in the basement. "We have to sell the house," I suggested to Jacques. "You sell the house," he said to me, "I'll take my share and live in Haiti."

Taking him at his word, I immediately contacted the agent who had sold us the house. In order to get a good price, I urged Jacques to finish the bathroom as quickly as possible: all the family members helped him carry out the work. Since it was a beautiful and large house, it sold quickly, but for a price lower than we had hoped. I told Jacques that I wanted to move closer to downtown or the surrounding areas: I would accept living in a small house since, with him leaving for Haiti, I would remain alone with the children. I would also accept him taking part of our furniture there. He then offered to accompany me during my house visits. I saw no problem with this and never once imagined that he was planning to set a trap for me. I finally found a modest house in the Villeray neighborhood, on Boyer Street. Since Jacques was self-employed, I agreed to let him co-sign the purchase contract, and my sister co-signed for us.

But when the time came to pack his things for Haiti, Jacques suddenly declared that he had changed his mind. He calmly announced that he had decided to live in the small house with us. He then added, "My decision is final. I have my plan. Don't forget, anyway, I'm the boss here."

The children, to whom I shared his reversal, seemed confused: "But it's way too small. Mom, where is he going to put his stuff?" I explained to them that there was nothing we could do about it anymore. We were dismayed.

It was Jacques who had freely decided to return to Haiti; in fact, he had constantly lied to me throughout this matter: he had misled me about his true intentions. The house had already been bought, I couldn't go back now. I was therefore overcome with intense feelings of anxiety and bitterness.

9 PM — I feel tired and my back and legs hurt. I've been sitting for too long. I stop writing and I'm going to take a bath. Goodnight volume 1

Ninth part

The death of Jacques' brother

The death of Jacques' brother. At the same time, we are facing all sorts of problems, we receive bad news.

At the same time, we are facing all sorts of problems, we receive bad news. Raymonde, Jacques's sister who lives in Philadelphia, informs us that their youngest brother, Frantz, is seriously ill and does not have much time left to live.

It seems that your message is empty. Could you please provide the text you'd like me to translate?

The different family members are then informed. Natatsha, for her part, hasn't returned yet. As soon as she arrives, I invite her to accompany me to the grocery store. On the way, we talk about everything and nothing. All of a sudden, I realize that I haven't revealed the news to her yet. "You know, Natatsha," I started, "your uncle Frantz is dying." She doesn't let me finish: "I'm glad," she immediately says. In front of my astonishment, she repeats: "I'm glad he's dead."

In front of my astonishment, she repeats: "I'm glad he's dead." At the time, she refused to justify her words.

At the moment, she refused to justify her remarks. Then, as I insisted, she told me: "If I tell you, you mustn't talk about it to my father." Without promising her anything, I reiterated my question: "What happened?" You have to tell me. She then dropped it, in a resigned tone: "He hurt me when I was little." — What? I shouted. — I shouted. — He abused me. He abused me.

He abused me. Under the impact of the revelation, I almost caused an accident.

Under the impact of the revelation, I almost caused an accident. After stopping the car, I urged her to tell me everything. Frantz had made her believe, she revealed to me, that it was a game and that she shouldn't tell anyone, so the game would remain interesting. She was five years old. She added, "He told me, even if you say it, your dad won't believe you."

She added, "He told me, even if you say it, your dad wouldn't believe you." I wanted to know why she hadn't told me before.

I wanted to know why she hadn't talked to me before. "Growing up," she explained to me, "I started to understand certain things." Moreover, there were sex education classes at school and conversations with my classmates. They also talked about it on television. I realized that it was not a game at all. At one point, I thought about telling you, but I knew my father would never believe me. — I believe you! I kissed her. It felt like I was watching the scene unfold before my eyes. I would have liked to strangle that man. His acts of sexual assault had been committed in Terrebonne while we were hosting him. He sometimes had custody of the children. At first, I had trusted him, but after my neighbor told me how he had courted her, I no longer believed in him.

At first, I had trusted him, but after my neighbor told me how he had courted her, I no longer believed in him. Upon returning home, I immediately went to see Jacques.

Back home, I immediately went to see Jacques. He was lounging in the hot tub. After informing him about Natasha's confidence, I strongly advised him to talk about it with his daughter. He never did. I strongly recommended that he go to Philadelphia to confront his brother on his deathbed. "Alright, I'll go next week," was his response. — No, go right now, he could die any day! He ignored my suggestion. Two days later, his sister called us to announce the brother's death.

Jacques never spoke to me about his brother again. And he never brought up the subject with his daughter, judging it probably too heavy to handle. He has clearly decided to act as if the issue were forever buried.

He has clearly decided to act as if the matter were forever buried.

The illness of my brother Robert

The illness of my brother Robert My brother Robert has always lived with my sister Irène, and he has been ill for a few years.

My brother Robert has always lived with my sister Irène, and he has been sick for a few years now. At times, his illness worsens: my sister then calls me so that we can take him to a hospital. Our cousin Viviane occasionally accompanies us. Very often, nearly an hour passes before our brother agrees to be taken to the hospital. It is obviously due to his illness, and not out of bad faith, that he adopts such behavior.

It's obviously because of his illness, and not out of bad faith, that he behaves this way. He is more receptive when Viviane is present.

He is more receptive when Viviane is present. My sister, on her own, never manages to convince him. As for me, when I go to pick him up in my own car, he says to me: "Ah! So, you're coming to pick me up in your Mercedes, like a big lady, thinking that I would agree to come with you!" And he bursts out laughing.

And he bursts out laughing. When he speaks like that, we don't react.

When he expresses himself like that, we don't react. Patience is then called for. We are waiting for him to decide to come out. I know that it is a very heavy burden for my sister to bear. At the beginning of her illness, we met with her doctor to consider the two possible solutions: placing him in a community center or keeping him at Irène's, and she agreed to keep him. I know that this arrangement is extremely taxing for her. I visit her regularly, and when she is away for one or two weeks, I go see him every day while bringing him dinner or supper, even though he doesn't really like it. He tells me every time that he can manage on his own. He is indeed quite independent, but I still continue to offer him my modest contribution.

A Sunday in Quebec (October 22, 2006)

6:30 PM It was a very beautiful Sunday morning. After breakfast, I went to the 9:00 AM mass. When I returned to my room around 10:00 AM, I sat down at the desk. I wanted to start writing again. I remembered that for years, I had often written in my journals or scribbled personal notes on sheets of paper, and then I thought it would be better to first organize my documents. So, I sorted them by month and year, then I carefully reviewed my writing plan. The whole operation took some time, but it was worth it.

At 12:15 PM, I went to lunch. A woman approached my table and asked if she could sit with me. I agreed. We talked about everything and nothing. She told me that she had come to take a course at the monastery.

She asked me why I was here. I told her it was to write. After lunch, I went back to my room to get my coat, intending to take a walk. The supervisor then called me to offer free foot care. The students, he explained, need volunteers to practice. I accepted, and the session was scheduled for 3:00 PM.

I took a stroll around the neighborhood. I walked for nearly 40 minutes. I returned at 1:45 PM. I wrote for an hour, just to relax. At 3:00 PM, I went to the place where the foot care was given. I enjoyed it, it did me good. The pedicurist noticed that I was beginning to have a fungal infection. After applying treatment, she prescribed a set of products to cure the infection. It was 4:10 PM when I returned to my room. I meditated and cleared my mind. At 5:00 PM, I went downstairs for dinner. Afterward, I went to the chapel for my evening prayer.

Before returning to my room, I called my sister to check on her. Upon returning, I changed clothes and sat down to write. It is now 7:00 PM. All in all, I think I will rest tonight. I'll do some reading in bed. Good night, and see you tomorrow.

Chapter 8

The Little House of Horrors, Boyer Street — June 1991

Monday, October 23, 2006, Quebec

Present Moment

9:20 AM. Hello, my darlings. I'm here with you. Last night, I didn't write about my past. I went to bed early. I wanted to clear my mind. I read something relaxing. But before I started reading, I felt the need to talk to you, Elle-Camay, and to you, Mikaël. Because, since I've been here at the monastery, I haven't been able to communicate with you. I learned from your mom that you were busy. You had your schoolwork, and you had to shoot in an American film.

When we talked, you gave me details, especially you, Elle: you revealed to me that the film featured a sexual aggressor. At the end of the filming day, each of you was given eighty dollars. Your mom told me that Mikaël bought a souvenir at Costco.

We shared that we loved each other. I was happy to talk to you because I missed it a lot. After that, during our conversation, I did a bit of reading. I was able to sleep around 10 PM. I slept well, but you know me: as usual, I dreamt a lot; my mind traveled all night.

I was in Miami, New York, and Montreal. I met cousins, friends, and strangers.

Every night, when I go to bed, I ask God to spare me nightmares. You know, I've realized that it all depends on how I spend my day. And also on what I wrote about my past.

Some nights, I'm afraid to go to sleep! I tell myself that with all I see in my dreams, I could write a work of fiction.

So, my dear ones, this morning, we're going to move on to another chapter of our adventures on Boyer Street, located in the center of Montreal.

You know that, since yesterday, I should have started telling you this part of my life. I wasn't able to. I feared hurting myself or suffering. Despite the moral strength I've gained since I started this story, I still feel a bit weak.

What I need to tell you relates to events about which I am in a fierce inner battle. Events I cannot reveal to anyone. My darlings, you are before me, with your mom Natatsha, and your dad, Max. I look at you through your portraits on my desk. You, Elle-Camay, you, Mikaël, you, Isaiah, you, Analysia, Aaliyah, and you, Samy, my dear little nephew. I see you smiling in front of Samy's beautiful birthday cake, so joyful and innocent about what life will bring you, without thinking about tomorrow, and without knowing how.

I must do my best to continue this journey, and it is through your joy and innocence that I must find the strength and will to continue telling my story.

So, here is the continuation of my adventure.

Part One

Moving into the Little House of Horrors on Boyer Street

Moving

Our family was well accustomed to the moving process. This time, it was extraordinary! In fact, packing up our belongings was a real headache, as over the years, we had accumulated so much! Because of Jacques' renovation company, he had bought many tools, both large and small, and had an entire stock of materials.

Oh my God! It was too much! I didn't know where to begin, my head felt like it was going to explode. And just by recalling these memories, I've had a terrible headache since yesterday. I can feel things jostling inside my brain in complete disorder, all trying to come out at once. Wait! Let me close my eyes to organize my thoughts. One moment! I'm here! Before I continue describing the move, I think it's better to first describe the little house of horrors. You'll understand why I've chosen this order later.

Let's start by describing the outside of the little house of horrors. In the front, a small fence touched the sidewalk. On either side of the entrance, there was a flower bed and a neat little treated wood gallery with a small roof. Also, on each side, there was a window with small square panes of varnished wood that gave a very charming touch to the little house. The front door was also made of varnished wood. Inside the entrance was the coat closet. On the left, you could see the master bedroom, not very large; on the right, my daughter's room, which was even smaller than mine. A hallway separated them. Right after Natasha's room, there were small, somewhat dark toilets with ceramic tiles that I found too dark for my taste. Exiting the hallway, you could see the kitchen, big enough to contain a small dining area. At the back of the toilet, a washer had been installed. Max's room was behind mine, which opened into the kitchen. It had no window. The previous owner had added an extension for a living room and another on the right side. He had also added a small two-story section, five feet by five feet, to make a storage room. The storage room, separated from the living room, had a small window and a door leading to the yard, through which you could enter without going through the house.

Now, back to the living room. It was about five feet long. It was really too small for what we intended to put in there. A five-foot-high basement contained the heating system: the rest of the basement only offered two feet of height, so it was impossible to store much, especially since it was made of rock.

The living room window overlooked Max's room and had no window for ventilation. The back door opened to a large yard that was twice the length of the house. The parking area was very spacious and could easily accommodate four cars. The rest of the yard was covered in grass. The yard was fully fenced, and a large gate opened onto the alley. You could see the other neighbors and watch the comings and goings of pedestrians in the alley. It was a beautiful little house just for the children and me, without Jacques, without his company and baggage, before it was transformed into a house of horrors.

I chose this house because it fit my budget, and the mortgage wasn't high. It was good. It hadn't cost me much, and I had put down a good deposit to reduce the mortgage, leaving me enough money to pay off our credit cards and settle other debts.

At the mere sight of the house, Jacques already knew he wouldn't be going to Haiti. He had left me to struggle on my own, and as soon as everything was settled, he came back in to declare that he was the boss. Well! We couldn't believe it!

The kids wanted us to take a spacious apartment for the family. I convinced them that it was better to buy a house so we wouldn't lose everything. I had a feeling that all our savings would have been spent in the blink of an eye.

And that's the description of the little house. The rest will come after my lunch.

A Return to the Present

12:45 PM I've just returned from lunch and am heading up the stairs. I'm rushing to continue my story, which I'm starting to find extremely captivating. I'm not taking any breaks; I'm diving right back into the task.

Another Reshuffling

We received a lot of help for the move. There were Max's friends, my brother Robert once again, and two of Jacques' employees. This time, he handled the move with his large trailer, which he had built himself.

My daughter Natatsha and my niece Marlène were also there to help. When the men arrived with the furniture, they placed it in each room according to its designated spot. When it came to the dining room furniture, however, that was a real problem! For the small one, it was fine, but how to arrange the larger one? Jacques stacked them one on top of the other in the kitchen. When the other furniture arrived, like the big TV, the living room furniture, the big desk, etc., he did the same thing, piling it one on top of the other in a corner of the house.

As for the boxes, I had labeled them before the move. We were able to place them in their respective spots. The children's boxes were placed in their room, and a good portion of mine (the most important ones) in my room: the rest went on the kitchen counter. Jacques' work desk was placed in the area that was supposed to be the living room. For the rest, there was no more space. "We'll put everything in the basement and deal with it later," Jacques decided. In reality, he was maneuvering to reserve as much space as possible for his tools and materials. "Faster! Faster!" he insisted to those helping us, acting like a real taskmaster.

Other items, like bicycles, the snow blower, the lawnmower, tires, etc., were left outside on a small wooden porch without a roof at the back of the house. He covered them with plastic. My God, it was dreadful! I didn't know what to do or what to say. The children and their friends were speechless. After I regained my composure, I told Natatsha and Marlène that we had to do something. I started by unpacking the boxes in the kitchen, and we then placed the dishes. We dismantled the dining room set and placed the pieces at the back, with the chairs stacked on top of each other. We did the same with the components of the small dining room to create some space to move around, since all these items were blocking the way. Once the boxes were emptied, I took them out to the yard to free up space. I did the same for the rooms.

In short, we worked almost like robots. The men were working outside and in the basement under Jacques' supervision, while I managed on my own with two girls. In the meantime, Mr. called me to show me where he planned to build a small shed. The next day, he indeed began building it with the help of his employees. This delayed me in my own tasks.

My absolute priority was to get the house in order because we were expecting a visit from two of Jacques' nieces, Margo, 16, and Violette, accompanied by her two children, a 5-year-old girl and a 3-year-old toddler. Their stay was supposed to last two weeks.

With a lot of effort and enthusiasm, the girls and I managed to tidy up the house somewhat. Some items were temporarily placed in the living room. At least the small kitchen and the rooms were ready and usable.

As for Jacques, he did indeed build his shed. He stored some tools in it while brewing the idea of building a garage and expanding the house. He was planning to make many changes. Of course, I had my reservations.

Second Part

Living in a Narrow House

Jacques worked almost all the time. It was summer, and he was picking up contracts; while carrying them out, he also worked on renovating the house, especially the exterior walls, while attempting to organize his tools that had been relegated to the basement.

Natasha's graduation party took place just after we moved into the small house. She was accompanied by her friend Patrick. Her aunt Irène, who is also her godmother, took care of all the expenses for the occasion. She had also made the beautiful red dress that Natasha wore on graduation day. My daughter looked stunning. Everything went well at the prom. When she returned, she was happy and had greatly enjoyed her evening.

At the beginning of July, Jacques' family arrived from Philadelphia. There were five of them, aside from Marlène, who was still with us to help. It was vacation time. The family was happy, and we anticipated enjoyable moments from an exciting adventure.

Natasha's small room had a two-compartment drawer bed. It was in this bed that the mother and her children slept. Natasha, her cousin, and Marlène slept in the living room. This arrangement suited them perfectly, as they could chat for a good part of the night. Marlène would tell horror stories to keep them awake. They had a blast.

Max was always busy helping Jacques with his renovation work, so his friends would come join him at the house after his workday. I was responsible for hiring employees, handling the company's accounting, and so on.

During Jacques' family's stay with us, everything went well, even with so many people in the house. Our budget had increased, especially due to the food expenses. The niece organized almost daily barbecues, big breakfasts, etc. I didn't mind because I wanted everyone to feel happy.

Since Jacques was working continuously, I was the one who went out with his family. His mother loved crabs, and she prepared them every evening. And every evening, after a good dinner and a bath, she enjoyed her crabs, washing them down with a good beer. She enjoyed it, and I couldn't do anything about it. After two weeks, she left with her children and one of her two nieces, Margo, whose mother was supposed to pick her up after two weeks.

I was completely exhausted. Maybe I had taken on too many responsibilities. The house was too cramped for the number of people staying there. I had to prepare lunch for Jacques and his whole team, keep the accounting up to date, supervise the employees, manage the budget, and so on. It was really too much. On top of that, Jacques began treating us with hostility again and showing disdain toward Natasha. He lavished affection on his little niece Margo, who kept him company all the time. He gave her pocket money, but not to his daughter. Natasha had found a job at a McDonald's restaurant. He forbade her from going to work, claiming she would use it as an excuse to "wander around."

On two occasions — Natasha's birthday and her graduation — I asked her father for money to buy her a gift. I was refused each time. "I don't give anything to a beggar!" he would joke. He humiliated us in front of his niece. Once, in my presence, he gave money to his niece so she could buy clothes at a street sale on St-Hubert. Natasha went with her. Margo snubbed Natasha and tried, through various hints, to show her that Jacques loved her much more than Natasha. My daughter didn't respond and pretended not to hear. When she told me about the incident, I urged her not to worry about such trivialities: the important thing is that I loved her and her brother.

As for the job at McDonald's, I eventually accepted Jacques' decision but made the following suggestion: "It's settled, Natasha won't go to work. But you should give her pocket money, because she wants to work just to buy what you refuse to give her. You should also take care of her as you're supposed to."

"That's not my problem," he retorted immediately. "I'm the boss here. Everyone has to follow my orders."

At that time, Jacques and his daughter fought almost every day, and the house became a real hell whenever he was present. One day, I remember it like it was yesterday, I was sitting in the living room. The computer and printer were in a corner on the desk. When Jacques returned from work, he immediately started yelling at me about Natasha. This time, I couldn't take it anymore; it was the straw that broke the camel's back: I grabbed the printer and threw it on the floor. It broke into several pieces, one of which injured my foot. I still carry the scar. "That's enough!" I screamed. "Let me live in peace!"

Jacques made up every excuse to go after his daughter. He even called my sister to badmouth her. Once, Natasha shouted at her father: "You never loved me! Remember what happened with your brother; you never came to see me to talk about it. By doing that, you showed me that you didn't trust me and that, according to you, your brother never committed that act!"

I intervened to tell him that I didn't understand why he hadn't gone to Haiti, as planned. Then, crying, I screamed: "Natasha needs to work!" And I added, "You're not the only boss here; there are two now!" Without responding, he abruptly went outside.

That was the end of the confrontation: Natasha went to work. During a weekend, we drove the niece back to her mother in New York. The rest of the summer passed quietly. Jacques did tell me, however, that since Max and Natasha each had a job, they should pay board. I agreed to avoid another dispute. But I made, without him knowing, other arrangements with the children.

Notes from My Journal

July 15, 1991

For some time now, I've been caught in an inner crisis that has drained all my strength to write. Life throws so many surprises at me that I don't understand anything anymore.

I have a husband I don't really know. And a daughter I don't yet know. I suffer a lot, and I don't know what to do anymore. I ask God to help me.

I hope I don't crack before then. I'd like to leave here to think and clear my mind because I can no longer think normally.

An Incident That Might Be Worth Telling

One day, I was alone at home, and a technician from the Videotron company came to install cable. He broke my VCR. I told him that he needed to replace my device. He refused, claiming that it wasn't his responsibility. Given the very tough moments I was going through at the time, I wasn't in the mood to tolerate this kind of setback. The technician arrogantly said, "Well, madam, do what you want, but you won't get any video equipment from me."

I asked him to call his supervisor, but he refused. "You broke my device," I sternly told him, "and you think you'll get away with it so easily?"

"What can you do about it?" he sarcastically replied. "You have no proof."

Grabbing a nearby baseball bat, I shouted, "Do you know, sir, that lately I've been through all kinds of hardships?" While saying this, I tapped the bat and alternated between staring at it and at his face. "You call your boss right now!" I continued, "Or else..." With a trembling hand, he grabbed the phone, contacted his supervisor, and explained what had happened, revealing that I was holding a bat and ready to strike him. Then, suddenly, he passed me the phone. In a calm voice, the supervisor promised to send another technician and send me a new device.

During our brief conversation, I of course explained the reasons for taking such drastic measures. When our conversation ended, I handed the phone back to the employee, who then wrote a statement admitting responsibility for the damage to my device, and that an equivalent would be provided to me within two days. The man then quickly left, occasionally glancing back.

The outcome of this ordeal brought me great relief. Jacques and the children, to whom I told the story when they returned home, laughed until they cried. The unusual incident had brought some moments of joy to the family.

Third Part

The Children at College; Natasha's Prize and Rex the Dog

And life went on. With the holidays over, Natasha was to attend La Salle College for fashion design training. Max, on his part, had finally opted for studies in interior architecture.

We had agreed to cover strictly school-related expenses, while the children would pay for their clothes and a few additional supplies. When their father learned that they had also bought some little novelty items, he got angry: "They have money for extras, let them cover the other expenses!" Since they didn't actually have the means, it was my sister who came to my rescue and paid the remaining fees.

Upon entering La Salle College, Natasha participated in a fashion contest and won a trip to Paris.

She came up with the idea to make a short dress, fringed and sleeveless, out of plastic garbage bags. As usual, I offered to help her, but she did most of the work herself, including drawing the dress. The plastic material was particularly difficult to sew. She had to wear the dress herself during a school fashion show. She left, fully convinced she would win — just like she was at every competition she participated in. "You always have to stay positive in life," she said.

Around noon, while Jacques was busy building a garage in the yard and I was updating my accounting, I heard the doorbell. Natasha stood at the door, beaming, hands full of gifts. "Mammy," she exclaimed, "I won all of this, plus a trip to Paris. When I found out I had won first prize, I was over the moon!" I hugged her and jumped for joy with her. I then went to share the good news with Jacques, but he didn't react. "Jacques, make an effort, go congratulate her," I quietly pleaded. Reluctantly, he approached her, kissed her on the cheek, and gave a faint smile. Then he went back to work. That was it. I never bothered to find out how my daughter took it; I was too outraged by Jacques' behavior.

When Max heard the news after school, he immediately rushed to hug his sister and congratulated her warmly. I then prepared a delicious dinner for her. My sister promised her some pocket money for the trip to Paris.

Max had made new friends at his college, and a few girls were now part of his circle. One of them, particularly kind, often came to the house. But in the end, it was one of his best friends that my son would marry.

Jacques and his Italian neighbor had become very good friends. One day, this neighbor, who spent his winters in Florida, offered Jacques his German Shepherd, a mean dog but well-trained. They first discussed the necessary acclimatization phase. "From time to time," the neighbor explained to my husband, "I'll let you feed him. He'll eventually understand that you're my friend, and then you can adopt him and finally take him home. After that, never let him off-leash."

Which was done. Jacques built a doghouse for the dog and placed it in the yard. I sometimes fed him myself. Max did as well. But we were very afraid of him and didn't trust him. Natasha never could get close to him, despite all her efforts to win him over, because she loved animals very much.

One of our neighbors, a young man, sometimes worked for Jacques. One afternoon, when his boss was absent, he unexpectedly came to the house to collect his paycheck. Venturing into the yard, he saw the dog in its open shelter and proceeded. The dog lunged and attacked the young man. He managed to puncture his pants and bit his backside. Jacques had to compensate the boy for the injury.

I later learned that the young man knew the dog well and had even "incurred a debt with Rex." As kids, he and his friends would provoke and irritate the animal through the fence of its previous owner; they would throw stones or wood shavings at him. He never forgot. As we know, dogs have long memories, just like children.

Back to School

Since I had already taken a secretarial course at C.S.M. College, I decided to further my studies in accounting and computer science by enrolling at Rosemonde College. I certainly wanted to improve my office skills, meet interesting and dynamic people, and so on.

It was an intensive and demanding course; I completed many assignments. And thanks to consistent effort and determination, I passed the course. I was planning to pursue university studies afterward, but I had to give up because I could clearly see many obstacles ahead, including a lack of time and a very unhealthy family environment.

Jacques had always opposed, for more or less clear reasons, the idea of the children having their own phone line. Suddenly, one day, he announced that he would allow them to have their own phone number. The next day, I made the necessary arrangements, and the children got their phone line. They were thrilled. But we were then caught in a trap, as I will explain later.

A Brief Break

It's 6:15 PM, I'm back from dinner. This afternoon, I was in such a hurry to have dinner so I could quickly get back to my writing that I arrived ten minutes earlier at the dining room. Usually, the nuns have dinner at 5:00 PM, while the boarders do so fifteen minutes later. I hadn't checked the time. When I entered the dining room, there were two of them. One of them reminded me of the meal schedule for the nuns and for the others. I apologized and then left to wait for them to finish their meal. The nun's reminder didn't bother me at all: I thought it was completely normal for the rules of the institution to be respected.

This observation applies to all areas of social life. I'm giving myself a brief break to recover. My neck hurts, and I can't concentrate; some stretching might bring me some relief. I'll be back shortly.

7:00 PM. I did 15 minutes of walking in my room and some stretching. I'm feeling better now. Let's continue with our story.

I will now tell you how a part of the small house was demolished. Pay close attention, as this step in my story is extremely painful.

Fourth Part

The Demolition and Renovation of the Small House

One of Jacques' employees, Maurice, was very experienced in home renovation. But he worked like a madman.

I knew that, although the house was small, we would have to make some renovations at some point. But I wasn't expecting such extensive work, nor for my partner to start it without informing me.

Before continuing, let me explain what renovations needed to be done. To put it simply, the house had a structure that stopped before the extension. This part was made of brick. Jacques was going to demolish it while respecting the support to enlarge the rooms starting from the extension.

Before going further, I want to describe as accurately as possible the transformation plan established by Jacques. The house had an annex. He planned to demolish it while preserving the basic structure in order to expand the rooms from the annex. He planned to move the bathroom, which was behind Natasha's room, to the left of the annex; place the kitchen on the right side of the annex, across from the bathroom, which would allow for a small dining area between the kitchen and the bathroom; move the wooden wall to install the dining room. The washer and dryer would be placed in the new bathroom, which would be large with an embedded shower and a small whirlpool bathtub. Max's new room would be located at the back of Natasha's room. He would enlarge the master bedroom, install a desk where Max's room had been. In the center of the house, a large living room and a wardrobe would be arranged. This was Jacques' renovation plan.

With the help of his employees, he immediately began demolishing walls; armed with sledgehammers, they worked like true madmen, spreading dust everywhere. The house, like many old constructions of the time, was made of slats covered with plaster. I hadn't covered the furniture. My God, the dust was overwhelming and unbearable! The air became unbearable. Each time I complained, Jacques would tell me, "Go to your room and let us work." And his workers would laugh.

He always did the demolition work at the end of the day, when he returned from work, without informing me. However, he quickly managed to bring everything down. Then, while he and Maurice were placing new support beams, the other workers moved the bricks, slats, etc., outside. On my end, I couldn't stop sweeping. Only Natasha's room was somewhat spared.

It was a Friday evening. With Maurice's help, he decided to work all night to finish the plumbing and install the bathroom. By morning, he was taking Maurice home. Then, with Max's help, he finished the plumbing on Saturday. The sink was placed temporarily, as well as a small built-in shower, because the tiles hadn't been installed yet. The washing machine and dryer were also installed.

Then he focused on Max's room. Max, eager to finish so he could enjoy a space free of dust, completed the room himself. After finishing the bathroom, Jacques worked on the plumbing, the kitchen, and installed an unfinished countertop with shelves that had no doors. The rest of the work was also completed without finishing.

We lived for a long time in this dust. The family atmosphere had become unbearable. Jacques resumed his arguments with Natasha after one evening, during an ice storm, when she had called us to announce that road conditions were preventing her from coming home. I accepted, but Jacques forced me to call Natasha's friend to demand that he bring her back, despite the bad weather and the poor road conditions.

After this incident, Natasha began to defy her father again. He then forbade Patrick from coming to our house. Patrick stood on the porch with Natasha and their friends. Whenever we had dinner and he was present, I would offer him food on the porch.

Despite my distress, I continued taking my classes at CEGEP and participating in meetings of the Miragoânais Association, which helped me clear my mind. I also sometimes attended meetings of a charismatic group with my friend Anièce; these were held in the basement of the Saint-Antoine Church on Beaubien Street, between Christophe-Colomb and Normanville streets, near my home. The association, which planned to organize a Saint-Jean-Baptiste celebration, was considering renting a cabin for the occasion. Jacques and I knew someone who owned one in Morin-Heights, and we had even stayed there a few times. The owner, once informed of the plan, kindly offered it to us for two days.

The cabin, overlooking a side, had a very spacious yard that extended down to the river. On the first day, several people chose to spend time by the water around a barbecue. Meanwhile, Viviane, my sister, and I prepared rice. People had fun, some dancing to very lively music, others swimming in the river. I took care of everything, ensuring things ran smoothly. It was when I went upstairs that I met the mysterious lover who gave me a sweet kiss on the cheek (I have already mentioned this incident in my first book).

In short, almost everyone was happy and in good spirits. Some found love; a child was even conceived in that cabin. It was wonderful to see the joy on everyone's faces. We reunited with friends we had lost touch with. And Viviane, who never stopped making us laugh with her hilarious jokes, enjoyed seeing people eat heartily. When food was running low, she would join my sister and another participant to prepare another pot of rice. Five minutes later, she would return with the pot emptied and jokingly say, "Look, there's no more rice in the pot, our friends ate it all, like Apaches!"

At the end of the day, after the revelers had left, Viviane and her two daughters, Jacques, my brother, and I stayed at the cabin to clean up. The next morning, we were ready to return to Montreal, satisfied.

So, while I endured painful family and marital trials, I did everything I could to create joy around me. This attitude helped me survive. During those times, I experienced a certain joy; just seeing my loved ones happy made me feel good.

Quebec

Tuesday, October 14: A Moment of Introspection

I feel very weak this morning; I had a restless night, unable to fall asleep. I felt a certain emptiness inside; nothing seemed right in my head. I didn't feel capable of praying or reflecting, even after having a mint tea. For a moment, I thought that sleeping pills could help me, but my doctor has forbidden me from taking them for years. Yesterday was particularly exhausting, my children, I probably pushed myself too hard mentally. But I know that despite everything, I must continue; and I pray to God for the energy and health I need. I don't like to dwell on my emotional states here, in the midst of this writing project. I don't want to worry you or alarm your parents and Aunt Irène. In the pages I wrote to you yesterday, I approached the material as someone preparing a cake by mixing several recipes. I imagine that if a philosopher or psychiatrist read my story and comments, they would probably underline everything in red.

Fifth Part

Christmas 1991

Due to the renovation work in the house, it was impossible to celebrate Christmas as we had before. We couldn't decently invite guests into a place almost buried under debris. Still, I decorated the living room with small decorations in the absence of a Christmas tree. The children received their gifts, which didn't stop my heart from being sad. In anticipation of each Christmas, I had saved a few dollars in a discreet place (a box), the secret of which only Jacques shared. It was partly thanks to taking cake orders and making pies that I managed to save this money. When we lived on Lamoureux Street, business was thriving. For every unexpected expense, I reassured Jacques, "Don't worry, I have the amount you need." When my Mercedes needed repairs, I had the necessary extra funds. But at one point, things started to go wrong: after my car accident, I stopped taking cake orders, so I couldn't save money like before. Money became scarce, and our budget shrank.

I still wanted to make my family happy, while also pleasing myself. I've always considered Christmas to be a sacred institution. All human beings should feel happy on this blessed day.

Winter was beginning to show its first signs, and Jacques worked less outside; he spent more time at home. But whenever I invited him to accompany me for errands, he almost always refused, citing the important repairs he was making to our residence. In reality, he did very little while constantly complaining about being short on money. I reminded him many times that I had advised him to take advantage of his profitable summer contracts to save up for the winter, but he had always ignored my warnings. Wanting to stay on the cutting edge of modernity, he constantly bought tools without caring about their cost. These tools were like toys to him. And he justified his incessant spending by repeating that he needed to protect "his little arms."

At the same time, he made sure I wasn't happy. Every time he saw me happy, he would use disgusting methods to ruin my good mood. He didn't like me reading, as it took me away from him! His manifestations of annoyance confused me, and it was only later that I would understand his true motivations.

As she did every year (since Terrebonne), my sister invited me, a week before Christmas, to accompany her downtown to shop and pick out my gifts. At the same time, she gave me a certain amount of money, with which I bought interesting presents for the children and a few bottles of drinks, in preparation for the holidays.

That day, I took 250 dollars from my secret savings box, leaving behind a 100-dollar bill. I placed the money in my handbag. I had informed Jacques the day before that I would be shopping with my sister. The next morning, after preparing breakfast and lunch for him, I told him I was leaving. He didn't react and didn't say a word. He just gave me a strange look, lips tightly pressed.

As I left the house, I had a vague feeling that my plan to go out was irritating him. But since I didn't want my day or my holidays ruined, I acted as if nothing was wrong.

My sister and I had agreed to meet at the Berri metro station. At this time of year, public transport is obviously the best solution. We shopped all morning. I chose a beautiful suit, including a navy blue skirt and a cream-colored silk blouse. I still have that suit.

We went to lunch at a large restaurant located on the eighth floor of the Eaton department store. In the early afternoon, we parted ways. I hadn't spent any of my money. When I got home, I opened my purse, and my wallet was there, but the money I had placed in it was gone. I couldn't understand it! I had kept my purse in my hands all the way through the metro; no one had touched it. I immediately called my sister. She didn't understand either. I told her I had saved this amount for small gifts for the family. After hanging up, I went to open my little "secret box." The 100-dollar bill was gone! I then asked Jacques if he had taken money from my box. "Oh?" he replied very calmly. Sitting in his armchair, watching a TV show, he didn't move.

I tearfully described to him what I had done the night before: taking the money from the secret box and placing it in my purse; the money had vanished. He didn't react. He pretended to find the show very amusing, but I could tell he was laughing at me, since the show wasn't funny at all.

I immediately called Irène and told her about the scene I had just experienced with Jacques. She immediately deduced that he was the culprit. That was also my opinion, and the children's. After all, he was the only one, besides me, who knew about the secret box. Reacting to the situation, I thought, "You won't make me have a bad Christmas." That year, I didn't give big presents to the children. Instead, I made small meat pies, wrapped them in gift boxes, and gave them to my loved ones. My sister, on the other hand, gave the children some money and told them to choose their own gifts.

On Christmas Eve, we attended midnight mass, after which the children and I went to visit my sister. Jacques, however, stayed in the car waiting for us.

On New Year's Day, my sister always hosts the whole family and a few friends. Jacques had warned me that he wouldn't be joining us. He remained inflexible, despite one of my friends' pleas.

So, we went without him, and we had a very pleasant day. That's how my first Christmas at the little house on Boyer Street went.

Help with Renovations

I've already pointed out that during the winter of 1991, Jacques got very few contracts. I had suggested that he finish the repairs in the house, but he told me he didn't have the funds necessary to pay his employees. "Max can help you, as well as our friend Dédé," I reminded him. Indeed, for two weeks, Dédé and Max pitched in and got the house in shape. With their assistance, Jacques made progress on the renovation and interior finishing work (the bathroom, the kitchen, etc.). However, there were still quite a few repairs left to complete, such as the floors in the living room, kitchen, and bathroom, the kitchen cabinets, etc. But at least my bedroom was finished.

Afterward, the house, finally somewhat livable, the work was halted for two weeks.

A New Break

11:50 AM. I can't concentrate to write. It's cold in the room. I'll take a break while waiting for the time. Outside. But I don't know what the temperature is exactly, because I don't have a radio.

Sixth Part

July 1992: Natatsha's Trip to Paris

By the end of spring, things started to pick up for Jacques. He was getting a lot of contracts, which excited him. It was up to me to hire the employees; the ones from the previous summer were back as usual. As for the new ones, I made sure to interview them before hiring. Among the employees, there was one who was always available, even during the winter when Jacques needed his services; his name was Justin. Occasionally, I made material purchases on Jacques' behalf when he was unavailable. My days were, after all, extremely busy. I had to negotiate contracts with potential clients and set the schedule for the work. I also handled the banking transactions, salaries, taxes, and accounting in general.

As soon as the snow melted, Jacques decided to build a garage. He didn't get a permit, ignoring my advice. He wanted to do things his way. With the help of his employees, he started preparations, working in the afternoon after his regular work hours. One day, we had a visit from an inspector. He asked for the permit. There was none. The inspector handed Jacques a booklet detailing the requirements for obtaining a permit. Jacques had to stop the garage construction in the meantime.

Among the conditions, one was to prepare a complete plan for the construction project. Max, who knew architecture, drew up this plan. Once the requirements were met, I went to get the permit myself. Needless to say, Jacques had to start all over again, this time following the construction standards. The garage ended up costing us a lot of money.

The extreme use of credit cards began again in full force. According to him, he would easily pay everything back by the next summer, thanks to his many and very profitable upcoming contracts. In the meantime, when money came in, he would push the payments back, citing other urgent expenses.

Natasha's trip was set for the end of June. She was supposed to stay in Paris for two months, but she came back before the scheduled date. When she left, I felt a lot of pain; the house was still a construction site. Everything irritated me, especially the clients who called to complain that Jacques hadn't arrived yet and that they had been waiting for one or two hours. Absorbed in building the garage, he disregarded my advice on keeping his commitments and respecting his clients. Sometimes, he would send me to supervise employees at a client's house; Max would watch another group, and he'd handle a third one. For me, the situation quickly became endless, as there was more work waiting at home: updating the accounting, cleaning, cooking, washing, and having sex in terrible conditions. In short, I didn't know where to turn.

One day, a client called again to complain that Jacques hadn't arrived. I couldn't take it anymore. I scolded him. He was obviously unhappy.

When Jacques returned, I shouted at him my frustration, "You're just doing your little renovation job. Here, I do everything, and sometimes, I even do your work for you. Tell your clients not to call me to complain anymore, because you're the cause of all the delays. I will no longer take the insults on your behalf." He turned his back on me without saying a word.

When Natasha came back from Paris, she told me she would return to work at McDonald's or anywhere else. Jacques, to whom I mentioned this, said Natasha wouldn't work that year. While we were talking in our room, I tried to explain to him that at 18, it was normal for our daughter to work. He stayed silent. But after leaving the room, he called Natasha. "Your mom told me you want to work, and I'll tell you right now that I don't want that, that's it," he decreed. This was followed by a pretty heated exchange between them:

"Well, I've decided to get a job. You don't give me a dime, and mom isn't in a position to give me any. Do you want me to tell you? You're not fulfilling your role as a father. If you don't want me to work, you should provide me with what I need."

"You have a roof over your head, you're well-fed. So what else do you need? Your real problem is that you only listen to your mother and your aunt, who are filling your head and encouraging you to go astray."

"Really, you don't understand anything; I'm 18 now. I have the right to make my own decisions. So, I'm going to work."

The exchange seemed to calm them down, and Jacques left. A few days later, Natasha indeed found a part-time job to gain experience in the job market.

Jacques was very jealous of the children, especially of his daughter. He didn't like to see us together, she and I. He thought it was unhealthy. He also disliked seeing the children hug me. "Yeah, yeah," he would say sarcastically, "Mom's precious little kids, the kisses, the hugs, yeah, yeah, yeah!" Yet, he never gave me any affection; everything happened in bed, his way, without any preliminaries.

Life at home was becoming increasingly unbearable. It was August. One day, during a run, I heard Jacques arguing with his daughter. Noticing my presence, she said, "Mom, I'm leaving the house, I'm going to get an apartment!" I asked her why. She didn't answer at first. Then, after a few seconds, she said, "I talked to Dad, and he ordered me to leave the house." I then asked Jacques for an explanation, and he told me it was better for everyone. "But I also have a say," I objected. Barely letting me finish my sentence, he shouted, "I don't want you to talk to me about this anymore! I'm the boss here! I want you to respect me! The subject is closed!" I pretended to continue the discussion, but he suddenly turned his back.

That day, July 13, 1992, my pain was so immense that I couldn't think or write about it. I still opened my journal, and here's what I managed to scrawl.

July 13, 1992

My God, I have to tell this story, I have to talk about it. Ah! It hurts so much. I have so much to say that I don't know where to begin or what to write. Oh, my God, help me.

End of Journal

My sister, to whom I had shared my deep feeling of being overwhelmed, promised to help Natasha find an apartment. After viewing several places with us, my daughter chose a modest place near Lafontaine Park and close to Irène's house. Jacques, with his trailer, moved Natasha's things. But throughout the entire operation, he didn't say a word and didn't enter the apartment. His attitude was like someone eager to be rid of his own daughter. Here are the reflections I wrote about this in my journal:

July 16, 1992

Natasha, my beloved daughter whom I love, has gone to live on her own in an apartment. She's 18, and she hasn't finished her studies. I'm very upset and happy at the same time. Let me explain myself better; I prefer writing my pain rather than talking about it or crying. I suffer because I've lost my daughter, my friend, and my confidante at the same time. I don't know what's going on with me. And today, I would like to be alone to think and meditate in peace. I would like to go far, far away.

The Aftermath of Natatsha's Departure

With Natatsha gone, I found my family and professional tasks, already quite heavy, increasing even more. My daughter was no longer physically near me, and I had no one to confide in as I had before. No one to support me in my moments of distress. I felt terribly isolated. But, on the whole, it was the best solution for her. The treatment her father subjected me to had revolted her, she had told me. Her new job at the perfume shop at the bay allowed her to pay her rent. She had also started working in hairstyling after initially wanting to study fashion design. She often came to visit me at home. She always said hello to her father, who always ignored her greeting. Over time, I stopped worrying about it.

The atmosphere at home, as I've said, was driving me crazy. Money was coming in, but Jacques continued his ruinous and extravagant spending. Fall was approaching. Jacques completely disregarded my advice regarding the need to save. He seemed, perhaps, to be getting used to the lack of money. He planned to spend the winter staying warm at home, doing nothing.

Seventh Part

An Offer for Miami

One evening in October 1992, I heard the phone ring. Jacques was at home. It was my friend Doris calling from Miami. Hurricane Andrew had caused considerable damage to her house as well as to my friend Josie's. Doris suggested that Jacques go there to do the renovation work. I discussed the idea with Jacques and my son Max, who found the offer very attractive. My partner and I then decided to work in Florida for the winter. Steve, an English-speaking friend of Max and an employee of Jacques, would accompany us. We agreed to set his salary once we were in Florida. My relatives were informed about the plan. We would leave in two weeks. I called Doris back to tell her our arrival date. In the meantime, Jacques worked on his truck, as we would travel by land, which would allow us to transport all the necessary equipment.

I prepared a list of instructions for Max to follow in my absence. I would send him money every month to pay the bills. I left a certain amount in the bank account. Max would have to take care of the dog, remove the snow, maintain the house, attend his classes at the CEGEP, and work part-time in the evenings. I knew I was asking a lot, but he still reassured me: “You know, mom, it doesn’t bother me as long as you’re okay over there.”

The trip was carefully planned. On October 21, we left with Steve. We stayed in New York for a night, then another night in a city near Washington. We arrived in Miami on the afternoon of the third day of the trip. It was a journey I would describe as both pleasant and exhausting.

Our Stay in Miami from October 1992 to August 1993

We found a desolate city. Roofless houses, houses without windows, abandoned. The further we went, the more horrifying it became.

Many houses, in fact, were no longer inhabited; disaster victims were living in trailers set up in front of what had once been their homes. They had been well compensated by their insurance companies once the inspection formalities were completed. The amounts granted were used to rent a trailer or a hotel room while waiting for their homes to be repaired or fully rebuilt— in some cases. Given the extent of the damage, there was a shortage of labor. There were fake contractors who disappeared with the money they were given and real contractors who were handling several contracts at once. Eventually, many of them also disappeared, leaving unfinished homes.

We were thus greeted with great relief. In addition to Doris and Josie, many other victims were vying for our services. Josie and her husband had taken refuge in a caravan parked in their yard. Doris, for her part, hadn't left her house; to replace broken windows, she had attached sheets to the windows and doors. Almost her entire family—her sister, her children, and herself, as her husband had passed away—was sleeping in the same room, as parts of the house were completely uninhabitable. Her friend Roline and her three young children were also staying with her temporarily (Roline's husband was working in the state of Maryland at the time). This whole group was defenseless against the mosquitoes, which feasted on them with great pleasure.

Doris had placed us in the least damaged room. To my great surprise, I discovered that Roline was one of my students from the time I taught primary school in Haiti. She had been informed of my arrival, but had made Doris promise not to mention it, of course, to maintain the surprise effect. Seeing her again brought me great joy. We became very good friends during my stay in Miami. On the night of our arrival, it was she who prepared dinner while Doris showed us around the house.

After dinner, we spent part of the evening talking about the aftermath of Hurricane Andrew. We then went to bed, as Doris had to work the next day, and we were exhausted from such a long journey.

The next day, Jacques and I began assessing the repairs to be made to the house so we could prepare the contract. We went to inquire about the material prices. Jacques then temporarily fixed the living room windows and the sliding door.

The following afternoon, my friend Josie and her husband came to greet us; they took the opportunity to ask us to give them second priority on our reconstruction schedule. Our potential clients were reassured and confident, especially since they had noticed that Jacques hadn't traveled alone (Steve, I remind you, was with us). They counted on us, for them, as if God had sent angels to save them. On my part, I was very happy to see that we were bringing them joy and hope. It was clear in their eyes.

Two days later, we presented Doris with the contract for the roof and window repairs; the clauses related to the subsequent work were also submitted.

At first, she seemed hesitant. Jacques then gave her a two-day deadline to let us know her decision. If not, we were ready to return home immediately. Meanwhile, other potential clients were eager for us to begin. Jacques then agreed to do small repairs at a lady's house. Seeing this, Doris finally accepted the contract and gave us a 60% down payment to start the work. The money would be used to buy materials and pay salaries (a new employee had joined Steve).

Thus, we were able to renovate several houses. We had to redo roofs, lay ceramic tiles, paint, redo plumbing, etc.

As the days passed, Roline became, as I've already mentioned, one of my best friends, and we always went shopping, grocery shopping, and running errands together. I encouraged her to get her driver's license and buy a small car.

One of the damaged houses was for sale. Very spacious, it had five bedrooms, two living rooms, a bathroom, a sitting room, two large toilets, and two sliding doors in the master bedroom, which overlooked a very large pool. The price was very reasonable, but it had to be paid in full. I called my sister to tell her I wanted to buy the property and ask for a loan. The request was approved. Doris also advanced me part of the amount needed. After selling the house a short time later, I managed to pay everything back.

Everything was going quite well. Jacques had obtained some additional small contracts, with the bulk of his work, of course, focused on Doris's house. The so-called minor repairs were done in the afternoons or evenings. The small team worked almost nonstop. Steve, for example, was always at work and was paid quite well.

One of Doris's neighbors was named Jocelyne. She lived with her mother and two daughters, one aged 6 and the older one 14. The father of the younger girl was Doris's brother. Jocelyne had become our friend, or more specifically, Jacques's friend. One morning, he told me he was going away for a few days with her, for business. She was, he explained, going to show him how to buy used cars to resell them for profit. He was really looking forward to this trip and left me alone with Steve to continue the work. His absence lasted a whole week.

It was the holiday season. We were supposed to return to Montreal in the last days of December. We planned to renew our passports to attend my aunt Dadia's remarriage (with her ex-husband), scheduled for January 3, 1993. I decided to return by plane with Steve, while Jacques preferred to drive the truck back. Upon my arrival in Montreal on December 22, 1992, everyone was delighted to see me again. The next morning, I went to the passport office, and they promised me I would receive them within a week.

Eighth Part

The Return to Miami — Dadia's Wedding

The Events During the Montréal - New York Trip

For the return trip to Miami, we organized everything meticulously. Several family members planned to attend Aunt Dadia's remarriage, including Natatsha and Patrick, who would travel in their own car, Viviane and her two daughters, Steve, Jacques, Max, and me. This whole group would first head towards New York, and then Max, Steve, Jacques, and I would continue our journey to Miami. Viviane and her daughters would return by car with Patrick and Natatsha.

The van was packed with tools. Max drove the Mercedes, which Jacques insisted on bringing to Miami. We crossed the Canadian-American border without any issues, but a few kilometers after the border, the van broke down. The fuel pump had failed. Jacques was confident he could repair it and dismissed our suggestions to tow the vehicle to the nearest garage. He immediately got to work. Meanwhile, it was freezing cold. At one point, noticing that Jacques was freezing, Patrick went to find him: "Don't stay out there freezing, come join us in the car," he pleaded. For once, Jacques listened. After sitting in the car, he could barely speak a word due to his numb lips. A few minutes later, he tried again to start the van, but in vain. Finally, throwing in the towel, he agreed to let Max get a tow truck. The van was towed to a garage. It had taken nearly 5 hours when he finally gave up. This incident clearly showed how stubborn he could be.

Once the van was repaired, we continued our journey to New York, where we stayed for two nights. After that, we left for Miami, with Max still driving the Mercedes. The day after our arrival in Florida, it was time to get to work: Max would stay in Miami for just a month before flying back to Montreal to continue his college studies. Doris greatly appreciated his efficiency and hard work.

A little later, we took possession of our own house. Jacques had managed to rebuild the roof, clean the interior, and remove the debris that was blocking the pool. The real renovations would be done later. In the meantime, we were occupying a reasonably livable house.

One evening, Natatsha called me from Montreal to tell me that she was coming back to live with us. I passed the information on to Jacques, who was entirely okay with it, as it meant Max wouldn't be left alone in the house.

My brother Raymond, who lived in Fort Lauderdale, was unemployed. Jacques managed to convince him to join our team while staying with us. One of Jacques's nephews also came to live with us. A month later, my friend Roline and her three children, who had been staying with Doris, joined our small colony. We gave them a whole part of the house. We were living together as one big family. Since I wasn't working outside the house, I had taken on the task of cooking. Since it was almost always hot, I mostly cooked in a simple swimsuit. Occasionally, I would jump into the pool to cool off from the intense heat.

Ninth Part

Marital Conflicts Resurface

I Return to Montréal

As the days went by, Jacques became very aggressive towards me again. It started as soon as we arrived in the new house. He would throw himself into mood swings and treat me very badly in front of the employees and our friends.

I was gradually losing my illusions. While living in Miami, I had hoped for an improvement in our relationship and the end of the pointless arguments. During the time we stayed with Doris, indeed, there had been very few clashes between us. All our loved ones called us the ideal couple, which didn't stop me from staying on my guard.

My friend Josie confided in me about her marital problems; she suffered from constant stomach aches. Here is the essence of what she told me: "Nouche (that's the nickname she gave me), you know, I've never told anyone about my troubles except you. To everyone, we appear to be a model couple, exemplary and all, but you have no idea what I endure! I always have stomach pains. Sometimes, I close my eyes and beg Jesus to come and take me away." I tried to comfort her, encouraging her not to lose hope and assuring her that everything would eventually get better for her.

I also shared some of my own struggles with her. She believed that only prayer could change things. Like me, she had two children, a daughter and a son, about the same age as mine.

We visited each other very often. And suddenly, one fine day, she told me that I could no longer come to her house. She was very upset about it, and so was I. "Nouche," she sighed, "you know I love you very much; you also know why you can't come to my house anymore." I reacted by nodding my head. I then tried to bring it up with Jacques, but he refused to discuss it.

He was trying, by all means, to subject me to a real dictatorship. When I revealed my extreme exhaustion and suggested a few days off in Montreal, he categorically refused. Yet, he had already finished several contracts, including the work on Doris's and Josie's homes. In his mind, it was unthinkable to stop. His construction business had become an obsession for him.

This obsession also had consequences on our sexual relationship: he made love to me with wild violence, and I experienced excruciating pain. Since I had a return ticket to Montreal, I made a reservation. Monsieur seized my passport as soon as I announced my departure. Out of caution and for security, I entrusted all my other identity documents to Roline. On the day of my departure, he refused to give me my passport and to take me to the airport. It was finally Jocelyne who took me there.

Upon arriving in Montreal, I immediately received a phone call from Jocelyne: she was also coming to Montreal for a three-day stay. I was completely confused. Why was she making this trip? It seemed mysterious and troubling, especially since she didn't know anyone in Montreal and it was her first time visiting Quebec. Accompanied by her daughter, she drove from Miami to Montreal in a jeep and stayed with me! Yet, it's Jacques, her friend!

I admit that, in some situations, it's better not to know too much... Jocelyne was Pentecostal, while I was Catholic. It happened that Jacques and I accompanied her to her church. I firmly believe that we all worship the same God, and He listens to our prayers wherever we honor Him.

Tenth Part

The Shock of Returning to Miami

When I returned from Montreal, Jacques agreed to pick me up from the airport. However, he didn't say a word to me. He just dropped me off in front of the house with Milly, Viviane's daughter, and Max, and then he went back to work.

When I opened the door to our home, I almost lost consciousness; the house was in a deplorable state. The pool was dry and dirty, the floor of the house was smeared and sticky. The fans didn't work. The kitchen and the bathroom reeked, having been left unattended. Cockroaches and flies were everywhere. But the worst surprise came from my bedroom: it looked as though someone had dumped a pile of trash in there. Dirty clothes were scattered over the chairs, the vanity, the floor. The bed was obviously unmade and disgusting. In short, the filth was spread throughout the room, producing an unbearable smell. The bathroom, which I had always taken such care of, was a disaster. I felt overwhelmed with sadness, disgust, and shame.

After the initial shock passed, I tried to reassure Max and Milly by promising that I would clean everything up quickly.

Then, taking a deep breath, I muttered to myself, "Jacques, you want to disgust me, don't you? Well, my friend, watch out!"

No sooner said than done: gathering my courage, I did a complete cleaning inside and around the house, except for the pool. I then prepared a large dinner because Max and Milly were very hungry. I was, too.

"Good morning, madam!" exclaimed Roline as she walked in. "The house is so clean! It smells so fresh!" I immediately asked why all the residents of the house had left it in such a pitiful state. She told me that, since I left, Jacques had ordered that no one touch anything in the house. "You must have noticed," she continued, "that my room and Raymond's room are clean." She added that, from the very first day of my absence, Jacques had emptied the pool and dumped trash in it. His children, her husband Francis (who had come to join her in Miami), and herself had stayed confined to their room. And despite the sweltering heat in July, Jacques hadn't put the pool back in working order. She couldn't understand how a human being could be so malicious.

After returning from the job site with my brother and his other workers, Jacques, seeing me in a joyful conversation with Roline, appeared surprised at my good mood. He was even more surprised to see that I had managed to clean everything.

We all had dinner together. When it was time to sleep, I set up a bed in the bathroom and locked the door. Jacques knocked, pretending he needed to use the bathroom. A little later, he knocked again, announcing that he wanted to talk to me. I refused to open the door both times. "You're my wife," he shouted. “I want you to come to me right now. I need to talk to you!” I replied, “Well, I have nothing to say.” After several more considerations, I finally opened the door and said to him, “You need me for sex, to keep mutilating my vagina. You just want to hurt me to get revenge. Know this: you’ll never make me endure these humiliating tortures again, or I’ll kill you. And I’ll warn you, if you try to rape me tonight, I’m going straight back to Montreal.” I was able to sleep peacefully in the bathroom for the rest of the night.

Since that fateful evening, he stopped torturing me in my body and private parts. I had had enough of enduring all that suffering. He also calmed down a little in his dealings with me. The day after the famous incident, without me asking, he cleaned and filled the pool with water in the late afternoon. The situation seemed to be improving, and I was happy about that.

By the end of July, my niece Yolaine, a doctor living in Haiti, called me from New York. She was about to give birth and had housing issues in New York. She asked if Jacques and I would take her in Miami. I discussed it with Jacques, who immediately agreed. Yolaine told me she would arrive in two or three days.

It was the height of summer. Max had returned to work in Miami with Jacques. I asked him to accompany me to find a public clinic that would take care of Yolaine. Fortunately, we found one in Key West. I described my niece’s case to the clinic staff. “No problem,” they told me. “Bring her to us as soon as she arrives here. She won’t have to pay anything for the consultation.”

I went to the airport to pick up Yolaine myself. She was happy to see me and told me she was seven months pregnant. Surprisingly, her belly had hardly grown. The day after she arrived, I took her to the public clinic in Key West. After examining her, the doctor gave her vitamins. Two weeks later, she was already feeling better, and her belly was starting to grow. She gave birth on September 13, 1993, to little Samy, whom I became deeply attached to. Unfortunately, I couldn't be there for the birth.

Montreal: A Sudden Retreat

The end of summer was fast approaching. Jacques and his employees were working hard. The maintenance of the house was causing high expenses. Meanwhile, I noticed that the attitude of our guests had changed significantly: hypocrisy had settled in. I told Jacques that it was time to sell the house and return to Montreal. "I will never live in Montreal again," he said. His response left me speechless. He was facing all sorts of difficulties getting paid by clients, with whom he was almost constantly arguing. We were struggling to adapt to the extreme heat of Florida, and now, he was revealing his intention to stay there permanently.

However, by a strange twist of fate, he suddenly became ill: he lost his appetite and grew weaker by the day. One morning, he lost consciousness. After helping him into the Mercedes with the help of my niece, I drove him to a medical clinic. Upon our arrival, he was put to bed. Diabetic, he was having a hyperglycemic crisis. In the afternoon, the doctor who examined him decided it would be better for him to return to Montreal. Once back home, I contacted my family doctor, Dr. Pavilanis. He advised me to have Jacques admitted to Notre-Dame Hospital immediately upon our arrival in Montreal, and he would get in touch with the hospital for the next steps. I then called my sister to inform her of the situation. Afterward, I made the arrangements for our return by air. Jacques's cousin's son would accompany us. Max, for his part, had already returned to Quebec to resume his studies.

Unfortunately, Jacques did not have time to recover the money—large amounts—that some of his clients owed him. My brother Raymond and Yolaine stayed in the Miami house for a while. And it was precisely because of our dramatic return to Montreal that I couldn't attend the birth of little Samy on September 13, 1993.

At Notre-Dame Hospital in Montreal, Jacques was immediately admitted to the intensive care unit. We left behind, in Miami, both vehicles, Jacques's full set of tools, the trailer, etc. Before we left, he had managed to park the van in the garage and store the tools there; the Mercedes remained in front of the garage. Out of caution, he had emptied the pool.

That's how we left Miami. If he had listened to me, things would certainly have turned out differently. We were in Florida in October 1992, intending to improve our financial situation during the off-season. But unfortunately, we returned to Montreal in August 1993, more broke than before and deeply in debt.

A Pause in the Present

Wednesday, October 25, 2006

10:30 AM Here I am again with you, my little ones! I just had a wonderful night. I woke up around 5 AM to the sweet smile of Natatsha: I was dreaming of her, and I felt good in my dream.

I feel very peaceful this morning. Yesterday afternoon, while writing about the time of my life I spent in Miami, I wasn't feeling very motivated. Part of me didn't want to relive that past. It holds too many secrets, and events that are so disturbing that I will never be able to reveal their true nature.

I don't know if you've sensed this blockage and resistance. There are events in life that are better left unsaid.

Eleventh Part

Jacques' Hospitalization

Jacques was admitted to Notre-Dame Hospital. He was in a private room, and I visited him every day. He hated being confined to a hospital. Relatives and friends would come in the evenings. He disliked these visits and ordered me to make them stop. He couldn't understand why I couldn't meet his demands, and he became very irritated. His constant bad mood was directed at me as well as the nurses. I was desperate. I often sought refuge in the hospital chapel to pray and sob. One morning, I brought him an image of the archangel Saint Michael. "Pray to him for your healing," I suggested. He tore the image into pieces and ordered me not to talk to him about prayers anymore.

One of the nurses on the floor, a Haitian woman, approached me one day. "Are you, his wife?" she asked. I nodded. She continued, "Why does he treat you like this? He is really cruel to you. Don't let him do this to you. He should consider himself lucky to have a wife like you who cares about his condition and comes to see him every morning. He should thank you every day."

She concluded, "You know, my dear, think about yourself. That's my advice to you." I pretended to agree, but at the same time, I made excuses to explain my husband's behavior. I was in deep distress and felt completely lost. To make matters worse, the doctors couldn't find the cause of his extreme weakness and lack of appetite.

His stay at the hospital lasted two weeks. On the few mornings I was slightly late, he would scold me harshly. He tried to inquire about everything going on at home. It was as though he was monitoring us from afar, even once making a scene with my sister on the phone from his hospital bed.

However, over time, he improved. Still, he felt weak and confided that he couldn't take a bath on his own. One morning, I took him to the bath. "You think I have no strength?" he suddenly said. "I'll show you I'm in great shape when it comes to what you know. Come here, give me what belongs to me." I resisted and struggled, pointing out that we'd be heard, but in the end, he got what he wanted and seemed satisfied. But I was not happy and warned him that he would have to manage on his own next time. He made me feel as though he was no longer in his right mind. No other explanation seemed conceivable.

From then on, I reduced my visits. He was now only focused on leaving the hospital. He had had enough and expressed his intention to the nurse on duty. "Sir," she warned him, "only the doctor can authorize your discharge." His insistence led them to call the head nurse. Fully dressed and ready to leave, he told her he was willing to sign a document releasing her from any responsibility. Reluctantly, she gave in. And he left the hospital, strutting like a rooster ready to fight.

I anticipated what would happen when we returned home: he immediately went to bed. I hesitated to follow, expecting what would come next. And what had to happen, happened: as soon as I lay down next to him, without any preliminaries, he violently mounted me as if I were an animal or a piece of furniture. The next moment, he was already asleep. I got up and went to sit in the living room. "My God," I sighed, "what awaits us, my children and I? How much longer can I endure these sufferings and humiliations?"

The next day, his sister Laura and her Protestant friend came over to pray for him. I tried to dissuade Laura, but she wouldn't listen. When Jacques came into the living room, his sister told him about her plan; in the meantime, she had placed a Bible on the table. Jacques lost his temper. Grabbing the intruder by the arm, he dragged her to the door, warning her never to return. At the same time, he threw the Bible onto the street. The scene left me completely petrified, but after a few seconds, I managed to recover and went outside to join Laura and try to calm her. She kept shouting at him that Satan had taken hold of his soul, chanting, "Hallelujah, Satan! Hallelujah, Satan!"

As Jacques pressed her to leave, she turned to me and pleaded, "Enice, you need to do something." After recounting the scene at the hospital to her, I promised I would try to reason with him, but I didn't guarantee anything. "Courage, my sister," she whispered to me before walking away.

"That's how I treat people who don't follow my instructions," he thundered when I came back in. "And I'll keep saying it; I'm the only boss in this house." I remained silent. While he continued in the same vein, I went back to my tasks, thinking about the uncertain future of my daughter Natatsha.

In the following days, he spent his time tinkering with electronic devices or watching television. I drove him to the hospital for his weekly medical treatment. The arrangement had been made after his premature departure from the hospital.

In an attempt to keep the peace, I became very small and complied with his whims. I had talked to the children, who agreed to be more careful. Meanwhile, my friend Roline, who was staying at our residence in Miami, had just bought her own house. After my niece's childbirth, she and her husband moved out, leaving behind my brother Raymond.

The Repatriation of Our Possessions

Jacques' condition had significantly improved. For financial reasons, we agreed that he would return alone to Miami to retrieve our belongings and put the house up for sale. To minimize the stress, he decided to fly.

He managed the task well, so to speak. After two weeks, he was back in Montreal. He had sold the Mercedes to a neighbor without informing me. The trailer, filled with our luggage, had been parked in his cousin Dophi's garage in New York. That was another problem solved. One of his former clients, a very reliable notary, had agreed to find a buyer for the house. And he did. The paperwork took about two months, and we had to travel to Miami to sign the deed of sale. I stayed with my good friend Roline during my time there. Thanks to the sale, our debts were cleared, including my sister Irène's loan.

We visited my friend Josie at her workplace (her husband, I remind you, had forbidden her from having me over at their house). It was a shock for all of us to see her physical condition; she was nothing but skin and bones. Unrecognizable, she looked pitiful. I felt immense sorrow seeing her. She confirmed that she was still suffering from stomach pain and that the doctors were at a loss as to the cause of her illness. I kissed her, and we cried together. We then renewed our vows of unshakable attachment and sincere affection. I promised her that I would continue praying for her. This encounter shook me. I nearly lost my voice, so tight was my throat from the emotion.

We returned to Montreal the following day. I learned shortly after that Josie was dying. Unfortunately, I couldn't visit her again before her death. She was in her forties. Her daughter later told me that Josie had a special thought for me. "Tell Nouche that I love her," she had whispered. After Josie's death, my behavior and my outlook on life changed profoundly. The following pages will clearly reflect this. I will never forget my dear friend Josie. I pray for the repose of her soul, and I dream of her very often.

A Pause in the Present

11:45 AM I stop writing. I wanted to check the plan for my writing project to take stock. It's time to go for lunch.

1:45 PM. Back from lunch. You know, while having lunch, I couldn't wait to return and continue telling you about my adventures. A lot of ideas were running through my mind. It was like little voices whispering to me: "Hurry up, we can't wait to know the end of this part of your adventures about the little house on Boyer Street!" I couldn't back out. So, I rushed, and here I am!

Twelfth Part

Life in the Little House on Boyer Street: Continuation

Natasha's Second Departure

Upon our return from Miami, we had a little money left. I paid the overdue months of our mortgage at the bank; I also settled all my arrears with the financing company Amco. I was determined to protect my sister's credit, as she had voluntarily guaranteed our loans. I then made a small payment on each of our credit cards, which allowed us to buy some time and hold on until our activities resumed.

We only had one car left, but we managed well enough since Jacques worked little outside. I received a salary every two weeks. The return turned out to be more difficult for him in the long run. He wasn't getting contracts, and our meager reserves were running out inexorably. Once again, I resorted to the credit cards to pay bills and repay debts. The longer time passed, the less money came in.

Aunt Nadia, who had come from New York, quickly noticed that my husband didn't show me any respect. She complained about it to my sister. During a meeting at Irène's house, we discussed the subject. They couldn't understand, as they insisted, how I could bear so much humiliation and cruelty. I replied that I didn't allow anyone to tell me whether I should or should not separate from my husband; the decision was mine and mine alone.

Irène didn't appreciate my attitude, but I had no choice. At that time, I wasn't thinking about the children's safety, as they were now old enough to take care of themselves, but about the loans that Irène had guaranteed. I figured that if I left Jacques, it certainly wouldn't be him who would continue paying the debts. I would be left to figure out how to get out of it.

Several times, I was tempted to ask for social assistance. But each time, a feeling of shame held me back. I will never forget those dark moments of distress. I cried and prayed. Then I asked Aunt Dadia to accompany me to a place, the name of which I kept from her. It was then that I filled out the application for assistance.

I felt extremely embarrassed describing my situation to the social assistance counselor. She explained that my request was perfectly normal. I received the income supplement I wanted that same day, with the promise that I would receive my first check the next day. The counselor also had me fill out a "disability application" for my husband, due to his health condition. I left the social assistance office with a light heart. But at the same time, I was aware of the fact that I was the only one facing all these responsibilities. I was taking care of Jacques physically (managing his diabetes treatment) and psychologically. I was also dealing, alone, with the financial burdens, those of the house and those of the company.

The checks from social assistance quickly proved insufficient. Jacques seemed to have a dual personality: when we were short on money, he showed no stress, but as soon as our financial situation showed signs of improvement, he turned into a real "coc," constantly starting fights. This is how, for trivial reasons, he started arguing with his daughter again. He would get angry when he saw me kiss Natasha. He would tell one of his friends what was going on at home and constantly badmouth us and my sister. He accused her of being the source of our family problems. Irène decided to talk to him and called him. Their conversation was violent, and Jacques said things that hurt me deeply.

His relationship with his daughter didn't improve; on the contrary. Since she didn't hesitate to speak her mind directly to him, he once again told her to leave the house. I intervened and yelled at him that I had as much right as he did, and as far as I was concerned, my daughter wasn't going anywhere. My statement made him furious, to the point that he started banging on the living room walls, not daring to physically harm us: Max was nearby, silently watching, never taking his eyes off Jacques. "If you don't want her to leave the house, figure it out!" he suddenly shouted. I didn't understand what he meant. In the end, Natasha didn't leave immediately.

Max had just bought a small family car, and since Jacques' truck needed several repairs, he, having resumed work, was using it to go to work. He was required to report his salary to the social assistance service so they could make any necessary adjustments to his monthly allowance.

Meanwhile, Jacques started playing all sorts of tricks on us. When Natasha did her laundry, he secretly poured motor oil into her clothes. When I wanted to borrow Max's car for my shopping, it mysteriously wouldn't start. I would then reluctantly ask for his help. He'd open the hood, mess with something, and the car would start. I was constantly forced to call him for help. Over time, he became the only one who knew how to make the car work. Suspecting that something wasn't right, I one day took the vehicle to Caron, Viviane's husband. Since he was a mechanic, he agreed to check it. Very quickly, he gave me his diagnosis: "Enice, your car doesn't have anything wrong, he chuckled. Someone just removed the starter. How did you manage to get it started?" When I told him that it was always my husband who took care of it and that he even suggested we get rid of the car because of its condition, he started laughing. Thinking back to the whole story, I still remember the incredulous expression on his face. Viviane, too, looked shocked.

Once he regained his composure, he told me that it was Jacques who had removed the part and offered to go buy a new starter and install it for me. In the meantime, I continued to think: "I'm sure the piece is in the car," I suggested to Caron. After looking around in the vehicle, I lifted the carpet in the trunk and found something that I showed to Caron. He immediately confirmed it was the missing part. He reassembled it, and the vehicle started on the first try. We were relieved by the resolution of the issue. But my sister, to whom we later explained everything, expressed sadness for poor Max, who certainly didn't deserve such treatment.

Back home, I casually told Jacques that Caron had detected the problem and found the solution. He didn't react. I then went to see Max in his room to discreetly inform him of what I had just learned. I also advised him not to park his car in our parking area anymore. Afterward, I never told my husband what I knew about his misdeed and his other tricks. What would that have served? To likely make the situation worse.

Natasha finally decided to leave — for a second time — because she couldn't take it anymore: the family atmosphere had definitely become too unhealthy. She found an apartment on Saint-Denis Street, close to us.

Business picked up again for Jacques. To better assist him on the administrative side, I enrolled in an accounting and IT course. Since I wanted to apply for a grant for the company, I consulted my financial advisor: I needed to participate in a training program. We did this as partners: Jacques as the entrepreneur and I as the administrator-accountant. After completing the training, I had to, under the supervision of a certified accountant, develop and write a business plan. Every afternoon, I would meet him at his office, and he would guide me through the process: identifying an issue, researching and interpreting statistical data, etc. One day, he told me: "Now you know what to do; build your business plan yourself, at home, using your computer."

Once the program was written, he reviewed it and asked me to make four copies: one for the company, and three to send to the grant service. Then he informed me about what would come next: "You and your partner will soon be called for an interview. In the meantime, he will need to familiarize himself with the plan's content so he can answer questions during the interview. Attention! You are two partners; if one of you doesn't show up for the interview, you won't get the grant."

I was really proud of myself. Back home, I handed the document to my husband. He seemed satisfied with the work, but he neither congratulated nor thanked me. His attitude didn't hurt me because I now knew my worth, regardless of his appreciation.

I then remembered that when I had received my first diplomas in accounting and secretarial work, he hadn't complimented me on those occasions either. I had simply treated myself by going shopping on Saint-Hubert Street. I bought those beautiful earrings I had been eyeing for a long time, then had dinner at an elegant restaurant. While thanking the Lord Jesus, I congratulated myself on my results and was very happy with my performance. Jacques, by letting me take those IT and accounting courses, wasn't thinking about me, I was well aware of that, but about the interests of his company. But I had pursued this for my personal fulfillment. And no matter what I take on in life, I remain convinced that I will always reap positive outcomes.

Thirteenth Part

Our Last Moments in the Little House of Horrors

The Circumstances of My Separation

As I write this part of my life, I must admit, my dear children, that I feel a tremendous pressure rising within me; I experience the same overwhelming sensation I had when I lived through these events. Back then, I sensed that something significant was about to change my fate, but I couldn't discern its form. I hurried to accomplish everything. It is in this same state of mind that I find myself today. As I've already mentioned, the death of my friend Josie in Miami had deeply saddened me. At the same time, it triggered a kind of awakening within me that I can't quite describe. No, there was no desire for vengeance, but a real and irreversible change: that was the effect the shock of the tragedy had on me.

The house was under renovation. I encouraged Jacques to continue the work that had been left unfinished. As he claimed to have no one to help him, I convinced Dédé and Max to assist him. Even though he knew I didn't like the black ceramic tiles, he had laid them in the bathroom, doing so as per his usual habit of always contradicting me. I no longer protested because I was tired of preaching in the desert. For the moment, what remained to be done was finishing the kitchen, installing the flooring in the living room, and so on—tasks he kept putting off. This didn't stop him from maxing out the credit cards, all in my name. He was constantly buying new tools, while I didn't even have a car.

Natasha had just informed me that she was pregnant; I promised to support her throughout her pregnancy. But when I told Jacques the news (after revealing it to Irène), he threw a fit: shouting and gesturing, he uttered the worst obscenities. He was aware of everything that was going on in the house, even though I hadn't shared anything with him. How did he manage it? By spying on all my actions, he constantly tried to restrict my outings. One day, my sister came to pick me up with Dédé to take me to the grocery store; according to him, I had gone to meet another man and was acting like a real prostitute. I tried to reason with him: "When you were sick, it was my sister and Dédé who supported me. Dédé is a precious family friend. He's always there for you in everything you do. Why are you so ungrateful toward him?" He was so angry that he didn't listen to me anymore.

Finally, it was spring. I had gained a little weight over the winter, and I had resolved to get rid of those extra pounds. My sister and I both signed up for a Weight Watchers program (she probably wanted to encourage me in my efforts); we would do our exercises once a week. Well, Jacques kept a close eye on us, watching to see if this weight loss program was just a ruse. Every morning, I went walking alone to complete my workout; he followed me like a shadow until I returned home. At the weekly weigh-ins, instead of losing weight, I was gaining it. Yet, I followed the program's guidelines to the letter. Irène offered a very plausible explanation: "You're too stressed, and you eat your emotions; that's why you can't lose weight." I decided to give up the program.

Held Hostage

One afternoon when we were alone at home, I heard Jacques screwing screws into the front door. I didn't pay much attention to it. A few minutes later, he repeated the exercise at the back door. "Enice, I'm not here!" he said before going out through the back door. Around mid-afternoon, I decided to run some errands. Simply. I opened the front door, or rather, I tried to open it. To my great surprise, I couldn't. I then tried to exit through the back door. Same result. "This is impossible! He wouldn't dare lock me in the house!" I immediately thought. The doors had been screwed in such a way that even if Max had returned before him, he wouldn't have been able to free me. Very upset, I called Natasha, who suggested I force one of the windows. I did so by breaking the one in the bathroom, the largest in the house.

After that, I went out. But since I couldn't get back in, I took refuge at my sister's place. A little later, I called home. Max was there, and after I told him what had happened, he told me that Jacques, upon returning, had opened the door.

When I returned home, I asked Jacques why he hadn't picked up the phone when I called. Ignoring my question, he gave me a silly, smug, and hypocritical smile. I couldn't take it anymore. I was at the height of disgust. I could have very well called the police when I was locked inside my own house. But I quickly dismissed that idea because he would have been incarcerated for a few days, after which he would have started an unbearable harassment campaign against me, depending on whether I decided to leave the house or not. I also thought about those heavy debts from his abusive use of my credit cards. And I felt overwhelmed with anxiety, fear, and painful resignation.

A brief but false calm followed shortly after. Max had a little English-speaking girlfriend who came to the house quite often, Yole. Jacques, on the other hand, spent most of his time in the garage, where he tinkered almost non-stop. He would only come home to wash, occasionally eat a meal, go to the bathroom, and sleep. Without our knowledge, he had installed an intercom somewhere: he was able to listen in on our conversations and those of our guests; he knew everything. In short, a real maniac, always on the lookout for dirty tricks.

Betrayal and Deceit

Jacques had been seeing a young woman in Haiti. She was now living in Toronto and was widowed. She called the house often and had long conversations with my husband. One day, he bought a cell phone for me, assuring me it would make it easier to reach him. In reality, it was to communicate directly with his ex-girlfriend without my knowing. At the time, however, no suspicions crossed my mind, even though I had noticed he was becoming more and more nervous. I sensed that another bad move was in the works.

It was Easter. He had planned a trip to New York and suggested that I accompany him. I agreed, while inviting Viviane and her younger daughter to join us. On the day of departure, she showed up with her daughter. On these occasions, Jacques was always a few hours late. To pass the time, we watched a television show while he pretended to do a final check on the van. It was 10 PM, and we were still hanging around in Montreal. Around midnight, he came to tell us he was going to rest and that we would leave at 2 AM. Viviane fell asleep on the sofa, and I continued watching television. At 9 AM, I woke Jacques up, and we finally got on the road an hour later. The wait had lasted nearly 17 hours, a record! He didn't speak a word during the whole trip, except once to ask if we needed to stop for the bathroom. At one point, he even opened his cell phone to have a long conversation with someone.

Before we headed to Aunt Dadia's, once we arrived in New York, we stopped by my brother Alain's place in Manhattan, and Jacques asked us to wait for him in the van while he spoke with Alain. This conversation lasted quite a while. Viviane and I were completely confused. When he finally joined us in the van, he seemed excited and had a mocking look on his face. "You took a long time," I remarked. "Do you have a problem?" He denied it but clarified that it was "personal."

When we arrived at Aunt Dadia's, she led Viviane and me into one of her daughters' rooms while Jacques went to rest in another room. "I have bad news to share with you," she began. Speaking quietly, she revealed everything: "Alain called me before you arrived to tell me that Jacques had recorded everyone on tapes, which he played for Alain. But he would prefer that you don't mention it to Jacques for now."

I was so stunned that I lost my voice. Viviane asked if "everyone" was included in this. "Of course!" Aunt Dadia immediately responded. "You, Irène, and everyone else." She continued, "Alain heard your voice and mine asking Enice why he was doing all this to you! Jacques thinks you're some sort of aimless person." Laughing, she added, "Jacques confessed to Alain that for several years, the entire family and all visitors had been under surveillance. He knows everything, especially everything about you, Enice." He had also told my brother that he wasn't afraid of any legal consequences because he had every right to find out what was going on in his own house. "Does Enice have a lover?" Alain had asked. Jacques had replied no and mentioned that he had happily played some of the tapes of an acquaintance of Irène.

I felt betrayed, defiled, ridiculed. In fact, these words imperfectly describe what I was really feeling. I stayed silent, but I wanted to scream my pain. As I write this part of my life, I feel overwhelmed with disgust for having endured all this torment without reaping anything. I went into Aunt Dadia's room and watched my tormentor sleep. A sudden and furious desire to kill him surged within me, but I resisted the temptation and prayed. I asked God to forgive me for the homicide I had thought of and to help me maintain my mental balance.

When he woke up, no one spoke to him about the matter. We acted as if nothing had happened. But he looked very proud of himself, as no doubt he was certain that he had pulled off another masterstroke. As for me, I maintained a cheerful appearance. We went shopping. Still, I was eager to return to Montreal to discover where that diabolical recording device was hidden. "In the meantime, Alain had informed Irène of the situation. 'Anyway, this is a real bombshell that has just dropped on the family!' he had told her. Max had also been informed during a visit to Irène's. Then, it was Natatsha's turn to be let in on the secret. During a small family meeting, we agreed on the conditions for using the phones. I should, on my part, secretly use the recording device behind Jacques' back. I didn't find it, but I discovered a small intercom. I had to continue my investigation and try to get my hands on the key that would give me access to the garage.

In the meantime, living under the same roof as this man had become unbearable. Despite the constant tension between us, not a night went by without him taking his dose of sex. Just the thought of the night approaching made me nauseous.

I thought I had to leave this house as soon as possible, but it was important to gather, beforehand, all the proof of my husband's trickery. I was holding back with increasing difficulty, feeling my blood boil with stubborn anger. The lid could blow off at any moment.

One Friday, it was past midnight, and my executioner still hadn't returned. Not knowing what to make of it, I dialed his cell phone number: no answer. I then tried to ask Max, but he hadn't heard from him either. Such a delay on his part—now it was 3 a.m.—was completely unusual. Suddenly, an idea came to me. I took a look at where he usually kept his small suitcase. It wasn't there. I also noticed that clothes were missing from the closet. "It's possible that during my absence, he got an urgent call from a close relative in New York and left hastily to go there," I thought.

The next morning, I called his cousin Baby, who ruled out any family emergency. And then, in the afternoon, he called me to announce that he was at his ex-girlfriends in Toronto and would return the following Sunday. He quickly hung up, not giving me a chance to say a word. I ran to my sisters to share the news. In no time, Viviane, Aunt Dadia, and Alain were informed. It was like a second bomb had exploded in the family sphere. The entire family was horrified, devastated. And poor Natatsha, who was carrying a baby at the time! I was doing my best to protect her from all this distressing news.

I returned home that Saturday evening, packed my bags without forgetting anything. But I hid everything to avoid him guessing my intentions. The next morning, Max managed, with the help of, I don't know what, to open the garage door. The recording device was there, on a shelf, hidden behind a box. So, this was the mysterious device that made him "skilled" and gave him that aura of apparent invincibility!

We tested the device. There was a phone in the garage. I asked Natatsha to dial my number from her own phone and hang up, and the tape recorder started working. Max's phone hadn't been tapped, but out of caution, we avoided using it. After taking some photos, we put everything back in place.

Jacques returned from Toronto in the early hours of Sunday. I was waiting for him, lying in my bed. When he came to lie next to me, I got up. I immediately revealed that I knew everything about the recording device; that he must not touch me, and that I was no longer his wife. His combative instinct quickly resurfaced. He was ready to explain why he had tapped our phones. The woman in Toronto was just a friend. Then, he tried to touch me; I forbade him. I tried to leave the room, but he stopped me and locked the door. He pleaded, “Darling, I want to talk to you, come to bed.” I didn’t give in.

I stayed for another week in the house. I was waiting for Max to finish his school year to help me move, and I was also trying to minimize the stress on him. He was finishing his college studies. His school projects and those of his classmates (painting, photography, sculpture, etc.) would be displayed, followed by a small reception. Jacques wasn't supposed to attend the small celebration because he was working that day. He had agreed to lend me his camcorder for the occasion. Sister Berthe and her companion, Sister Marie Marthe, Irène, Natatsha, and all of Max's friends were invited. I was filming when we saw Jacques arrive, much to our surprise. After greeting Sister Berthe, he offered to continue filming.

I stayed a little longer at the event. Max had offered to take me and my guests home, but we declined his offer; we preferred to take the metro. Throughout the journey, my problems with Jacques were the only topic of conversation. I acknowledged that I was going through very painful moments. "It's your life," my sister reminded me, "you are the only one who can decide what is good for you or not."

Irène got off the metro before us. After her departure, I described my state of mind to Sister Berthe: "It's true that Jacques has made me endure a lot of horrible things. There is a part of me that hates him to death, but at the same time, I feel pity for him. He asked me to give him another chance. I think I will, because he came to the reception tonight and his presence made Max happy. I believe this is proof that he really wants to make amends." After listening very attentively, Sister Berthe advised me not to force things but to still listen to my heart and pray urgently to God to help me make the right choice. We then parted ways, and before returning, I bought a bottle of wine at a convenience store.

When I arrived, Jacques wasn't at home. But that didn't matter! I felt so happy. I had just made the decision to give him one last chance, and I was preparing to announce it to him. Noticing that the phone's light was blinking, I picked up the receiver and here's what I heard: "Hello, Enice, I am 200 miles from Toronto, I don't know when I'll be back." That was all. I suddenly felt completely disarmed. Desperate and completely crushed, I called my sister to tell her what I had just heard and experienced. I refused her invitation to come to her place and told her I would leave the house as soon as Jacques returned. I also told Max everything, who had just come back, and I warned him that we would be out of there as soon as possible. "Mom," he then confided, "if I've stayed here all this time, it was only for you, to protect you." We hugged.

The next day, I told Natatsha the news. My sister agreed to store my luggage at her place, but we agreed that I would stay at Viviane's for two or three days to avoid Jacques harassing me. Max would spend some time at her place. Since he worked on Saturdays and Sundays evenings, he asked his girlfriend Yole to keep me company for two nights. Yole slept in the living room, and I slept in Max's room.

Jacques returned on Saturday night around 5 a.m. After turning me over in my son's room, he leaned over me, whispering, "Come to your bed, don't sleep here. Don't forget that you have back problems." Now, he was suddenly concerned about my back! "Go away," I screamed, "I'm leaving tomorrow morning. All my bags are packed. I've even booked a truck." He knelt down, begging me not to leave the house; he would accept that I sleep alone in our room, while he would now occupy Natatsha's room. I immediately cut him off. "Jacques," I said, "the night before last, I came home with the intention of giving you a second chance, as you asked me. But I found the house empty and I listened to the message you left me. That message hit me like a bomb. I didn't even know when you would be back. So, this time, it's really over between us! Go sleep in your bed; I'm staying here."

When the day broke, I took a shower, then had breakfast. Around 11 a.m., Max's friends came to help him with my move. And on Sunday, June 5, 1995, at noon, Max and I left the little house of horrors on Boyer Street. This date will forever be engraved in my memory. During the move, Jacques stayed there watching me, occasionally risking some intimidation tactics. But he no longer had any hold over me. A significant chapter of my life ended right there.

Continuation of Chapter 8

Thursday, October 26, 2006, in Quebec

Writing Journey of Volume II

A Moment in the Present

10:15 AM It's been sunny for the past two days. Although the weather is very pleasant, I haven't taken advantage of it to even go for a short walk. I content myself with admiring the beauty of nature through my window. The sunlight reflects on the river, creating rainbow-colored hues. It's truly fascinating and soothing. In front of all this beauty, I say a prayer to God, asking Him to continue protecting you. I also think about your parents, family, and all the people on the planet.

During the three days when I was writing about the adventures I had with your parents in the little house on Boyer Street, I didn't do any exercise! I only climbed the stairs from the basement to the third floor, and in the mornings, upon waking, I did some stretches in bed.

I was extremely eager to write this part of my life, and my thoughts flowed out of my mind, rushing to escape like customers in front of a seasonal sale. To regain some calm, I went to the chapel, prayed, and meditated. When I returned, the task felt difficult again, but suddenly I managed to control my inspiration. It was like I had to climb a huge mountain. There were many obstacles, and at times I feared I wouldn't make it. I worked like a possessed person.

I suffered from insomnia, nightmares. The characters haunted my sleep during the first few days I wrote Chapter 8. I prayed to God to send me an angel of light and peace. Then, I saw my daughter smiling at me with a gentle expression of peace on her face. The third day was the hardest. I was excited, but at the same time, I managed to control my emotions. Anyway, I had little choice.

I was so eager to accelerate my writing that I thought about skipping lunch. To avoid bringing back my anemia, I decided against it. I went downstairs to eat, hoping not to meet anyone. I quickly ate my lunch, so I could get back to work as soon as possible. I was completely immersed in the past. I was living it entirely. I had to do this to finally come to the surface.

Last night, when I reached the top of the mountain, it was 9:30 PM. I thanked the Lord. I then called my sister to announce the good news. I also called your mother, who was very happy for me. She congratulated me saying, "Mammy, I'm very happy for you. You did a great job, first for yourself, but especially for Max; it will do him good to revisit the past. He needs it to free himself and fully engage in life."

I told her that it was for her too. She immediately replied, "You know, mamy, that I am very strong in spirit, and it's you and Max who have been most affected by this situation." And she added, "Don't forget that it's not over. Don't let go, I will keep praying for you." Then she asked if I wanted to speak to my grandchildren.

Mikaël, I address you first. – You told me you're looking forward to seeing me. – You also told me you were waiting for me on Saturday. When I told you I would be back on Sunday, you were disappointed. We repeatedly said that we love each other.

And you, Elle-Camay, we just greeted each other, and then you whispered to me, "I'm waiting for you, grandmother." And I reminded you that I love you. It did me good to talk to the family. I needed it.

I must tell you that what helped me a lot in my writing activity was drinking water. I drank a lot of it. I filled a bottle each time I went to the cafeteria. This high-water consumption also helped me do a cleansing cure at the same time.

My daily shower is sacred. It's my usual vitamin. It gives me all the energy I need for the day. Again, the presence of water.

After talking to the children, I prepared to go to bed. Since I couldn't fall asleep, I decided to do a bit of reading. I arranged my five pillows in a way that would make me comfortable. When I arrived here, there was only one pillow on the bed. I took the other four out of the wardrobe in the hallway. I placed them as follows: one under my leg, one on each side of the bed, and the other two under my head. I had the good idea of bringing my little long, soft cushion. To feel more comfortable, every time I wrote, I did the following: I opened the drawer of my very small desk and placed the cushion there to support my arms.

I wanted my legs, feet, and back to enjoy maximum comfort. So, I put a pillow folded in half under the desk to rest my feet on and moved the desk closer to the bed so I could easily change positions if needed. I could rest one of my feet on the bed's rail. On my desk, just in front of me, were the photos of my loved ones. I felt complete. Don't forget that I had to spend fourteen days writing. If I didn't make sure I had this essential comfort, I would have had to say goodbye to writing.

After settling into the bed that evening, I began to stare into space. I didn't want to think about anything. I was like in a trance. I saw nothing and heard nothing; only the beating of my heart, which I found a little irregular and too fast. At times, ideas tried to break through. I stopped them: "No, not tonight." I wanted to preserve my peace. And without realizing it, I was overcome by sleep. I was suddenly woken up by a very violent cough. Just one, which seemed to try to suffocate me. In fact, I had just had a terrible nightmare: people were chasing me, and I was struggling in all directions. It reminded me of the scenes I had described yesterday regarding the little house of horrors. It was horrible and terrifying.

To calm my agitation, I took some water. I turned onto my side, but I feared falling back asleep. Ten minutes later, I went to the bathroom. When I returned to my bed, I lay down with my little cushion under my arm like a protector. I finally fell asleep, my little ones, as you know my nature well, I dream every time I close my eyes, even during the day. So, I began to travel in my sleep.

I will allow myself to tell you one of my dreams. I'm telling you this because I think it has meaning, it's a revelation.

In my dream, I saw myself as I am now. But I had lost weight. Natatsha was waiting for me at an exhibition. I think she had a booth. There were several people. They were watching me, but I didn't pay any attention to them. I went to find my daughter; she was in a good mood. A certain gentleman, one of the characters from my first book (Tony), was following me everywhere.

I pretended not to see him. I approached the counter to pay. Another man, whom I didn't know, came to congratulate me: "Enice, you know, I think you look great these days. You've lost weight and you look healthy." I thanked him and went out to get my car. The first character was still following me; he also got into his car. I didn't feel afraid. "I think I'll change direction," I thought to myself. But at the parking lot exit, there were two paths. On the right, the road was paved.

That was the one I was supposed to take. He knew it too. Since I had decided to change direction, I hurried and, without him seeing me, I took the left path. But this path was unpaved, causing a thick dust cloud. I intended to lose him and return on my steps to wait for my daughter at the exhibition. However, I couldn't continue, as the road ahead of me was blocked. I turned back on foot, but when I got there, I realized that I didn't have the first volume of the book in my hand.

I entered the exhibition hall. I noticed that no one was there except my daughter, who was still at the booth. Mikaël, you were with your father, both surprised to see me return. I expressed my intentions to you: "You will wait for me here. I'll go back to get my book." And I immediately went back on foot on the same road.

Back at the location, I didn't find the book, but I saw two men. One, sitting on a stone, was flipping through a book. Close by, there was a cliff; the other man was standing near the edge of the cliff. His feet were only held by two stones. The book lay at the bottom of the cliff. The stranger pretended to go down to get it. Approaching the edge, I exclaimed: "My God, I have to get my book, but I'm afraid of heights." I felt like I was going to fall. I realized that it was the man who had been following me. He shouted, "I'm going to fall!" I replied, "I can't do anything for you!" I thought that I, too, should not fall. So, I abandoned the book and decided to return to the children! When I arrived, Natatsha, Patrick, and Mikaël, I saw that you were waiting for me.

In my opinion, the meaning of the dream can be summarized as follows:

I had written my first book, *A Woman Among Many*, with the intention of leaving that part of my life behind. When it fell off the cliff, it symbolized, to me, that I had successfully moved on from that past. Just as the character from the book who had been following me had fallen off the cliff.

As for the other character in my dream, the one sitting on a stone flipping through a book, his presence meant that I would soon finish the second volume of my book; he, too, would disappear into the cliff, and that part of my past will also be left far behind me.

When I returned to the exhibition, I saw that my children, grandchildren, and many others were waiting for me. This means that my work isn't finished. I still have to write a third volume, which will be the last before crossing the border.

12:20 PM I'm taking a short break to go to lunch. I'll be back in a few minutes to continue the adventure. To continue our adventure.

Quebec, Thursday, October 26, 2007

Situation setup

Last night, I finished recounting 19 years of my life. My goal was to restart the story in two volumes. But at the end of the second volume, I realize there is so much more to tell, and I conclude that a third and a fourth volume are necessary.

I discussed this with my daughter, who agreed with me. She considered the idea of writing a third volume to be completely natural. So, I begin today.

Tales of a multifaced life, written by Enice Toussaint.

It is the second Volume of four Volumes published by

ENS Publishing

Éditions Nouveau Siècle.

For information, contact Natatsha Casimir

Visit our website: www.enspublishing.com

Email: ediontionsens@gmail.com

www.ingramcontent.com/pod-product-compliance
Lightning Source LLC
Chambersburg PA
CBHW071155070526
44584CB00019B/2806

* 9 7 8 1 8 0 6 2 3 7 1 4 2 *